STAGING STRANGERS

Staging Strangers

Theatre and Global Ethics

BARRY FREEMAN

McGill-Queen's University Press
Montreal & Kingston • London • Chicago

ISBN 978-0-7735-4951-7 (cloth)
ISBN 978-0-7735-4952-4 (paper)
ISBN 978-0-7735-4953-1 (ePDF)
ISBN 978-0-7735-4954-8 (ePUB)

Legal deposit first quarter 2017
Bibliothèque nationale du Québec

Printed in Canada on acid-free paper that is 100% ancient forest free (100% post-consumer recycled), processed chlorine free.

This book has been published with the help of a grant from the Canadian Federation for the Humanities and Social Sciences, through the Awards to Scholarly Publications Program, using funds provided by the Social Sciences and Humanities Research Council of Canada.

McGill-Queen's University Press acknowledges the support of the Canada Council for the Arts for our publishing program. We also acknowledge the financial support of the Government of Canada through the Canada Book Fund for our publishing activities.

Library and Archives Canada Cataloguing in Publication

Freeman, Barry, 1977–, author
Staging strangers : theatre and global ethics / Barry Freeman.

Includes bibliographical references and index.
Issued in print and electronic formats.
ISBN 978-0-7735-4951-7 (hardcover). – ISBN 978-0-7735-4952-4 (softcover). – ISBN 978-0-7735-4953-1 (PDF). – ISBN 978-0-7735-4954-8 (EPUB)

1. Theater and globalization – Canada. 2. Theater and internationalism – Canada. 3. Multiculturalism in the theater – Canada. 4. Theater and society – Canada. 5. Intercultural communication in the performing arts – Canada. 6. Race in the theater – Canada. 7. Ethnicity in the theater – Canada. 8. Theater – Canada. I. Title.

PN2301.F74 2017 792.01'3 C2016-906843-9
C2016-906844-7

This book was typeset by True to Type in 10.5/13 Sabon

For Jodie and Oliver,

and for Audrey and Owen Freeman

Contents

Illustrations

Acknowledgments

The preparation of this book depended on the tremendous support of my family, colleagues, and students – most of all, that of my wife, Jodie Bond, whose love and generosity with her time and energy made writing this book possible. Thank you as well to my young son, Oliver, who helped me by punctuating every exhausted hour with moments of pure joy and theatrical absurdity.

I have been blessed with supportive colleagues at the University of Toronto. Thank you foremost to my former PhD supervisor, now colleague and friend, Kathleen Gallagher. It was in conversation with Kathleen that I found language for an ethical perspective on theatre. Also at the University of Toronto, thank you to my mentors Michal Schonberg, Paula Sperdakos, Stephen Johnson, and William Bowen, who have done many things over the years to open up the mental space that writing this book demanded. And thank you to other colleagues whose work has been an inspiration: Veronika Ambros, Bruce Barton, Joel Benabu, Melanie Bennett, Antje Budde, Nikki Cesare Schotzko, Nancy Copeland, Xing Fan, Jeff Gagnon, Karen Gilodo, Catherine Graham, Alen Hadzovic, Nicholas Hanson, Sherri Helwig, Hartley Jafine, Matt Jones, Ric Knowles, Peter Kuling, Will Kwan, Trisha Lamie, Laura Levin, Shelley Liebembuk, Michelle MacArthur, James McKinnon, Scott Mealey, Burcu Yaman Ntelioglou, Jimena Ortuzar, Richard Plant, Jessica Riley, Denis Salter, Birgit Schreyer Duarte, Marlis Schweitzer, Kim Solga, Jenn Stephenson, Larry Switzky, Mumbi Tindyebwa Otu, Tamara Trojanow-ska, Lynn Tucker, Mark Turner, Anne Wessels, Robin C. Whittaker, Lydia Wilkinson, and Kevin Wright.

Thank you to my editor Jonathan Crago at McGill-Queen's University Press for taking an interest in the book, to copy editor Jane McWhinney, and to the excellent staff of McGill-Queen's. And thank you to my personal editor, Kathryn Allan, for her willingness to push my ideas farther.

Thank you to all students in the theatre and performance studies program at the University of Toronto Scarborough campus and University of Toronto's Centre for Drama, Theatre and Performance Studies. Many of the ideas in this book have drifted through my classrooms, where they were taken up, challenged, and revised. Special mention is owed to my theatre and globalization classes at the Drama Centre and my advanced seminar classes at UTSC over the last five years; these groups of brilliant people have taught me a great deal. I am indebted to those students who have been my research assistants (and sounding boards) over the life of this project: So-Jeong Choi, Dave DeGrow, Natalie Frijia, Matt Jones, Johanna Lawrie, Marjan Moosavi, John Rowntree, Jenny Salisbury, and Jay Smith, all of whom brought something valuable and different to the project. Every day I think about what an extraordinary privilege it is to talk with these inspiring people about the things I care about.

Thank you as well to members of the nonprofessional theatre community who so warmly welcomed my interest in their work. At Nové divadlo especially Jana Fabiánová and Dasha Hübschmann; and at the Chinese Opera Group of Toronto especially Angela Chu (chapter 2 was to include discussion of Chinese opera, but I now plan to take this up separately). I am also grateful to Robin C. Whittaker, who lent expertise on nonprofessional theatre, and as well to James McKinnon, who responded to an early proposal for the project.

Others provided valuable resources along the way, some of which made it into the final text and some of which became part of the learning process behind the book. Thank you to Cornelia Persich at Theatre Ontario, Vicky Gélinas at Statistics Canada, Cathy Leekum and Pasang Thackchhoe at the Multicultural History Society of Ontario, and to Davorin Cikovic at the CBC Archives (although Czech immigrant and important Canadian artist Jan Rubeš receives only a momentary mention in the book, his story was important in an early draft, and Cikovic's unearthing of recordings of Rubeš's glorious 1950s CBC Radio program *Songs of My People* was one of the happiest moments of my research).

Last but no less important, thank you to the many theatre makers I discuss in this book, especially Betty Quan, Catherine Hernandez, Ins Choi, Nina Lee Aquino, Daryl Cloran, Ahmed Ghazali, Matthew MacKenzie, Jovanni Sy, Mumbi Tindyebwa Otu, the Debajehmujig Storytellers and Nové divadlo. I hope this book will extend the conversations these artists started with their work. Sadly, a longtime member of Debajehmujig, Joshua Peltier, a member of the Global Savages ensemble I discuss in chapter 5, passed away from a sudden illness in April 2015. Josh was a larger-than-life, funny, and multi-talented individual who is a much-missed member of both Debajehmujig and the Wikwemikong community. Josh's loss only makes us more painfully aware that theatre is a life's work. I hope that this book, even in its most critical moments, serves to enrich and vitalize the theatre work we feel called to do today.

PROLOGUE

Strangers at the Threshold

You show up at the theatre, not sure what to expect this time. You are led out onto a street corner and left alone. It is five o'clock on a weekday afternoon in downtown Toronto and people are rushing about everywhere. A passerby tells you to walk down an alleyway and then disappears into the crowd. In the alleyway you are approached by a young man wearing a clerical collar. He introduces himself as James, chats with you for a short while, and pulls you into a busy laundromat. He tells you he has been keeping a routine of visiting the laundromat in the hope that he will again run into an unforgettable stranger he met there recently. James is chatty and charming, and before long he starts asking you a series of personal questions about your life. His manner encourages you to speak honestly and openly, but you are aware that he is an actor in a performance. So you have a choice: *Will you answer as yourself or play a character?* James sends you out onto the street with a wish that you too will meet an unforgettable stranger today.

In fact you are going to meet a number of strangers in a series of similarly brief and intimate encounters on the crowded streets. In one such encounter, you are walking in a park when you are spotted by an "old friend," who turns out to have been more than a friend in the past. She leads you to a tree in the corner of a park, flirtatiously cozies up close to you and proposes that you rekindle your relationship. *Will you give her a second chance?* In another encounter, this one indoors in the secluded basement corridor of an old industrial building, two women sit you on a chair and, from a distance of about an inch on

0.1 Promotional image for DopoLavoro Teatrale's *The Stranger*.

either side of you, whisper a monologue into your ears about the difficulty of making important life choices. They get you to follow them as they sprint through a labyrinth of corridors. When the corridor divides into two, the women take separate paths. *Which of them will you follow?*

In another interaction, you are given an iPod and ear buds and a saccharine pop song is played to you as you walk down the street. You meet a stranger who is evidently listening to the same song, and who leads you in a synchronized dance that has you skipping, frolicking, and running your hands through a public fountain – all in front of puzzled onlookers. *Will you play along?*

Such were the choices you would have been faced with as a participant in *The Stranger*, a performance created by the international theatre collective DopoLavoro Teatrale in collaboration with several Canadian theatre artists and first staged as part of Toronto's Summerworks Theatre Festival in August 2014.[1] Before attending, I knew nothing about the performance, and was attracted exclusively by its title. I had already been writing this book for some time, and "the stranger" had emerged for me as a guiding metaphor for characters somehow marked as culturally "other."[2] *The Stranger*, however, at least on the surface of it, didn't "stage strangers" as representatives of cultural difference. Its strangers were not marked as "strange," but were anonymous people in the street who could in an instant become deeply familiar. But what stayed with me was the way the performance so powerfully presented its audience with difficult ethical choices *without* dealing with difference.

The choices I was invited to make in this performance seemed designed not to reveal things about strangers but to have strangers reveal things about me. For instance, the penultimate encounter of the piece, with a young woman seated at the base of a statue in the middle of a broad avenue, became an occasion to imagine an alternative persona for myself. When the young woman asked, "What is your name, but not your real name?" and "What do you do, but not what you really do?" I played along but, quite exhausted by that point, I half-heartedly invented the alter ego of John the plumber. She interrogated "John" and, dissatisfied with his answers, accused him of lying about himself, launching us into a discussion about the difference between "lying" and "playing." Unimpressed (or perhaps bored?), she sent me off into the street again, where I was stopped one final time by another stranger, who asked me for directions to the subway. Only when he handed me an envelope addressed to the just-invented "John" did I realize he was an actor. The envelope contained a white masquerade mask and a handwritten invitation to a second part of the performance, to take place a few days later. In the intervening days, I was encouraged by email to create a Facebook profile for "John" that would connect me online to other "strangers," presumably alter egos for fellow participants in the performance.

When I showed up at the theatre for Part Two of *The Stranger*, wearing the mask from the envelope as instructed, I was greeted by actors and fellow masked participants. I looked for clues as to whether I was expected to be myself or John. None were forthcoming. I milled about awkwardly, grabbed a drink, and was eventually led onto the stage of the theatre for what I only later understood was the second part of the performance. Left alone, standing in the middle of an empty, dark stage and lit by a spotlight, I was played a recorded monologue – possibly James's voice – that riffed on ideas about masks, truth, and deception. A single performer wearing a suit and tie circled around me, holding a mirror in front of his face at such an angle that my own brightly lit features were superimposed over his body. The image completed the gradually accumulating impression left by the performance: that "the stranger" was in fact myself.

The impression that "the stranger" may stand in for both the "other" and the "self" – both "out there" and "in here" – is typically produced by the participation of a stranger in performance; the stranger is a complex and contradictory figure, simultaneously inside and outside the boundary of an imagined community, recruited willingly or not into that community's effort to define itself. In contemporary social theory, the metaphor of the stranger has been taken up in multiple discussions, sometimes in elaboration of the French philosopher Emmanuel Levinas's idea that to see the "face" of the stranger is to have an ethical obligation to that person, sometimes in relation to the Polish sociologist Zygmunt Bauman's sociological ruminations on Levinas's ideas.[3] While "the stranger" might be a device for discussing many kinds of difference, in this book I think of the stranger mainly in terms of cultural difference. This is how the idea was first introduced into critical theory by the German philosopher Georg Simmel, who was fascinated by the liminal position of actual strangers in his cosmopolitan, turn-of-the-nineteenth-century Berlin. In an essay still popular among sociologists, Simmel discusses the stranger as a figure who is no longer a wandering foreigner likely to disappear (usually a merchant hawking goods from distant lands) but a figure who, he writes, "comes today and stays tomorrow." Anticipating the approaching age of intercultural mixing, Simmel thought of the stranger not as distant and shadowy, the object of moral disdain or xenophobia, but as a figure who demands sustained attention and reconciliation with the moral community.[4] This insistence on inclusion, for Simmel, overturned the idea that the stranger was "out there." In encountering the stranger, he wrote, "he, who is close by, is far, and strangeness means that he, who also is far, is actually near."[5] The stranger was "here" to stay.

Strangers exist – and perhaps can only exist – at a threshold. As Richard Kearney and Kascha Semonovitch put it in their *Phenomenologies of the Stranger*, a meeting with a stranger is a theatrical encounter:

> The place where we encounter the stranger is a threshold. Quite literally, I might greet a stranger who comes to my door, and in

> that space and time discern something about this potential guest. Metaphorically, we can see "thresholds" defining the edges of human beings in many ways: for example, I find a threshold at the limits of my physical body, a threshold of pain, of pleasure, a threshold at the limits of one culture and another, one political group and another.[6]

It is the stranger's position at the threshold that distinguishes the stranger from the *neighbour* – who is nearby and may share certain values or belong to a shared community – or from the *other*, who has been marked as "outside." In this view, the stranger appears at the threshold of some kind of "home," a guest hoping for hospitality. What, in this encounter, becomes the "home" and who its "host," positioned to extend that hospitality?

DopoLavoro Teatrale's *The Stranger* illustrates how our thinking about the stranger has shifted in the century since Simmel wrote his essay. What feels dated about Simmel's theorizing today is its facile determination of inside from outside as well as its unquestioned notion that the "in" group is bound together by common values that the stranger can never possess. "The stranger is by nature no 'owner of soil,'" he wrote, "soil not only in the physical, but also in the figurative sense of a life-substance which is fixed, if not in a point in space, at least in an ideal point of the social environment."[7] As much as his theorizing of the stranger may have anticipated later postmodern theorizing of the "other" and "othering," Simmel wrote from a nineteenth-century European vantage point from which identity was inseparable from birthplace or nation. More recent theorists have uprooted the stranger and challenged Simmel's assumption of fixity of character or values. Kwame Appiah and Zygmunt Bauman, for instance, see the stranger as the agent who disrupts a fixed system of communal identity in the modern world. In his book *The Globalization of Strangeness*, Chris Rumford suggests that the way strangers may identify across less visible communities today makes it more meaningful to speak now of "a more widespread state of *strangeness*, a development which is of equal if not greater importance than the changing nature of the figure of the stranger."[8]

The Stranger was a vivid illustration of strangeness as a condition; every element of the performance was calculated to maximize uncertainty and to destabilize orientation in an otherwise familiar urban environment. Its momentary encounters with characters who held up a mirror to the participants perhaps unwittingly presented the stranger as a talisman of anxiety and fear or, in Rumford's words, as an "index of the fragility of social bonds and community sentiment."[9] Here the performance seemed to cast the stranger as a symbol of modern alienation in the context, as Bauman discusses it, of a cultural "stranger danger" that makes public space something to be feared. Or it could perhaps be said that *The Stranger* offered its audience members a brief respite from "stranger danger"; that is, if it can be argued that we have become alienated from one another, we can appreciate the satisfactions of a performance that stages individual public encounters charged with meaning. The performance curated surprising and intense flashes of intimacy within the unknowable mass of the urban mob. At any moment, it proposed, the stranger could become a friend, a fellow conspirator, or a former lover.

Having participated in *The Stranger*, I was disappointed by its suggestion that the stranger was in fact me. This, and other ways in which the performance cultivated a sense that it was "all about me," seemed to forfeit the possibility of really "knowing" strangers. And if the stranger had to be me, then what of *actual* strangers? In retrospect, I saw that this aspect of the performance pointed to a key dimension of my book – that discussing the theme of the stranger necessarily becomes a discussion of the "who" or the "we" called upon to look at, know, care for, or welcome the stranger into some community that is imagined and realized in the encounter. In this manner, as Rumford counter-intuitively suggests, the stranger can be usefully understood as "the study of ourselves and our 'we-ness.'"[10] DopoLavoro Teatrale's *The Stranger* thus addressed, perhaps inadvertently, the ethics of how difference is made to appear or disappear in theatre. In terms I will explain in my first chapter, *The Stranger* was ethical insofar as it asked its participants to make challenging personal choices about what to say or do. It may not have been ethical, however, to the extent that ethics involves meaningful confrontation with difference. This ambivalence is captured in Rumford's statement that the stranger's appearance "can lead to new forms of intimacy *and* new forms of indifference."[11]

In this book I use the stranger as a guiding metaphor for an analysis of cultural difference in theatre in Canada. I am concerned with how, why, and with what relationship to audiences the stranger appears within the swirling ideological currents of nationalism, multiculturalism, and globalization. By looking at examples that span several decades, I consider how the near and distant stranger has been staged in "immigrant theatre," in "multicultural theatre," and in a "theatre of global ethics." I consider how multiculturalism created a "politics of recognition" in which the stranger became a source of cultural affirmation, and look at the ways in which ethical relationships proposed between the local and global, the stage, and audience are realigning in a global context. By examining various strangers onstage in relation to multiple discourses of difference, I ask: what are the possibilities and limitations of theatrical encounters with strangers?

STAGING STRANGERS

1

Making a World of Difference

Theatre is going global. Stages that once were platforms for voicing local stories now commonly feature stories about distant places and issues as well. Take, as a paradigmatic example, Toronto's Cahoots Theatre Company, founded in 1986 by Beverly Yhap with a mission "to provide a much needed home for the voice of the 'other,' a place for marginalized artists and diverse communities to share their stories."[1] In its early years, Cahoots helped playwrights such as Daniel David Moses, M.J. Kang, and Rick Shiomi get their work produced and escape what some at that time referred to as Canadian theatre's "workshop ghetto" in which "visible minorities" (the term popular at the time) were trapped.[2] Early Cahoots productions focused on the experience of first- and second-generation immigrants: for example, Marty Chan's *Mom, Dad, I'm Living with a White Girl* and Kang's *Noran Bang: The Yellow Room*. In those plays the family was portrayed as a site of a confrontation between tradition and modernity, the old world and the new. About a decade ago the company started to take a more explicit interest in works about global issues. In 2007 it co-produced Ahmed Ghazali's *The Sheep and the Whale*, a play set on a cargo ship adrift on the Strait of Gibraltar that examined the global problem of forced immigration. Jovanni Sy's *A Taste of Empire* (2010) was a primer on the history of colonization in the Philippines and the corporatization of food production. Matthew MacKenzie's *SIA* (2012) told the story of a young Canadian volunteer taken hostage by a Liberian ex–child soldier in a plot to influence a war crimes trial at the International Criminal Court (a story based on MacKenzie's own research in a Liberian refugee camp in Ghana). Its productions of Nina Lee Aquino's *Every Letter Counts* (2013) and Kawa Ada's *The Wanderers* (2014), set partly in the Philippines and Afghanistan respectively, each in its own way addressed intergenerational conflict.

Cahoots's shift toward more global stories reflects a wider trend toward more globally oriented methods of play creation. Toronto's Volcano Theatre, led by Ross Manson, and Why Not Theatre, led by Ravi Jain, for instance, have both developed new works in collaboration with foreign artists; Theatrefront has created new plays through exchanges in Bosnia and South Africa; and Christopher Morris of Human Cargo researched his play *Dust* in Pakistan and Afghanistan and is working with artists in China and Israel on new projects. There are plenty of other examples across Canada, particularly from Pangea Arts and the Firehall Arts Centre in Vancouver and Teesri Duniya Theatre in Montreal. Despite the tendency to think only of major cities as centres of globalization, some of the most interesting theatrical forays beyond Canadian borders have been led by rural companies. Prime examples are the Debajehmujig Storytellers on Manitoulin Island in Ontario, and Théâtre Parminou in Victoriaville, Quebec, each of which has developed theatre projects with partners in Europe, Africa, and South America.

This project of this book began with my observation that this global shift was pressuring theatre to renegotiate its ethical relationship to near and distant strangers.[3] Multiculturalism seemed somehow to have made way for a different kind of globalism, and the implications for theatre had not been thoroughly considered. I became interested in how representations of strangers had changed, and how these new representations might differently implicate audiences. To use "the stranger" as a guiding metaphor for difference, I thought, is to position someone or something else as "not strange," a "host" in the position to "welcome" or "empathize" with strangers, part of a seeing, knowing or caring "we," who are members of ... well, members of what? An audience, yes, but what audience? A certain kind of "public"? A nation? A moral authority? "The West"? I have been fascinated by the ways in which I, as an audience member, have been called upon to see, know, or care for strangers. By looking at how strangers are treated – whether created in and through encounter, celebrated or challenged, made objects of fear or desire, domesticated or fetishized

– I offer here a variety of perspectives on how theatre in Canada "makes a world of difference."[4]

Since this shift toward the global can be observed across Canada, I use the phrase "theatre in Canada" to describe the general field of practice I am speaking of. But, despite the fact that my examples are mainly drawn from Toronto, many also connect out to other places. For example: the festivals I describe in chapter 2 were provincial and national in orientation, and the theatre company on which I focus is importantly international in orientation; the plays discussed in my third and fourth chapters all deal with the experience of immigrants and travellers, and most have been performed elsewhere in Canada or internationally; and one of the theatre groups I focus on in chapter 5 performs around the world. What "theatre in Canada" does not much include in this book, though it is a worthy and large subject, is any substantial take on the cultural politics at play between Anglo and Franco Canada; nor does it treat in any substantial way how the politics and ethics of the "intercultural" theatre play out uniquely in Quebec. My hope is that my argument for a theatre that carefully and meaningfully stages strangers, rooted as it is in Toronto, will resonate with other contexts. This introductory first chapter lays a foundation by assembling an ethical perspective on contemporary theatre in relation to several discourses of difference.

TORONTO, "WORLD CITY"

Before I flesh out an understanding of ethics in relation to theatre, I want to say a few words about Toronto as a special context for a discussion about difference. I have drawn my examples from Toronto partly because it is where I have lived and worked for two decades, but primarily because the city is a place where cultural difference has played a major role in shaping public discourse and the institutional practices of art and culture. Toronto is – or so it likes to think – a multicultural city like no other. But I would situate my discussion somewhere between, on the one hand, Toronto's aspirational cosmopolitanism, its self-mythologizing as a diverse city, and, on the other, the social realities experienced by its residents.

Torontonians will be familiar with the often heard claim that the city is "the most multicultural city in the world," a boast first made publicly in a 1989 speech by then mayor Art Eggleton. The expression quickly spread[5] and continues to be cited within the city and internationally.[6] In 2001 Toronto-based geographer Michael J. Doucet convincingly debunked the claim by demonstrating that Eggleton was exaggerating a United Nations report that had said only that Toronto was "one of the most multicultural" cities. Since then, Toronto's diversity has become less extraordinary as all cities in an urbanizing world have become nodes in a network of global diasporas. New York, London, and Hong Kong have higher ratios of foreign-born residents, and Toronto is on a par with a list of other cities in the world. But this has not supressed the city's desire for some kind of civic distinction; even as he debunked the claim, Doucet himself hoped it would be supplanted by another more "authentic" one, such that Toronto could continue to "claim a place near the pinnacle of the urban hierarchy."[7]

In any case, Toronto's diversity has evolved into a key dimension of its meta-performance as a global city today, its currency in a competition of what Michael McKinnie has discussed as the "civic transnational."[8] Toronto's 2011 official "Cultural Plan" frames diversity as a point of attractiveness to tourists and investors;[9] its (failed) bid to host the 2008 Olympics foregrounded the city's multiculturalism in its slogan, "Expect the World";[10] and Panamania, the cultural programming associated with the 2015 Pan-American Games in Toronto, had a mandate "to promote Toronto's cultural diversity, including its Aboriginal cultures and Canada's official languages."[11] The knitting together of diversity and economic well-being has also been championed by urban studies theorist Richard Florida, whose argument that a city's economic success correlates with the vitality of its "creative class" has been embraced with zeal in Toronto. When Florida moved to Toronto in 2007 to head up the University of Toronto's Martin Prosperity Institute, he spoke of his new city's potential to become a "first-tier mega-region," and a city spokesperson suggested that to Florida's prescription for a successful city – the three "T"s of Technology, Talent, and Tolerance – "we should add a fourth: Toronto."[12] Ironically, Toronto has not excelled in the Martin Prosperity Institute's "Global City Ranking," in 2013 placing twenty-fifth in the world and only seventh in Canada.[13] Out of the ranking's forty-one categories, Toronto was awarded an "A+" in only five, three of which were "religious diversity," "visible minorities," and "multiculturalism."[14]

Of course, for many Toronto residents the boosterist rhetoric of diversity does not square with the realities of life. The city is rife with experiences of social alienation, precarious labour, and unequal access to opportunity. Immigrants to Toronto face great obstacles in terms of access to quality of life and professional advancement. Though visible minorities constitute about 40 percent of the city's population, they occupy only 14.5 percent of high-level management positions of influence (a disparity that is even greater in Vancouver).[15] Many immigrants find their foreign training and credentials unrecognized in Canada, and polls conducted over the last two decades reveal that they also continue to experience prejudice and racism.[16] The lack of access to affordable housing in the city has long been spoken of as a crisis, with the waiting list for housing now including a staggering 100,000 families.[17] Toronto has a growing class of working poor, who are priced out of living in the centre of the city and must rely on an underdeveloped transit network to get around. For reasons such as these, cultural diversity has become less a feature of the city proper than of its suburbs.[18]

These realities demand an ethical consideration of discourses of difference such as "diversity." "It is increasingly urgent," writes Canadian theatre scholar Ric Knowles, "to come to a better understanding of how communication happens across difference, and how representation normalizes, 'others,' and 'disappears' its objects."[19] Being careful about how we discuss difference involves a healthy skepticism about such meta-concepts as the "global city." The British geographer Doreen Massey has suggested that a preferable alternative to the "global city" may be the "world city," which she describes as being rooted in a different geographical imaginary and a relational conception of space. Whereas "global cities" compete with one another for investments and tourism dollars and struggle to achieve this abstract status, Massey suggests that "world cities" are interdependent and constituted locally through internal and external relationships. Her notion of the "world city" emerges from her observation that in the UK, as in Canada, the multicultural fantasy sometimes obscures the reality; Londoners' pride in their multiculturalism, she notes, has them "turning a complete blind eye to the fact that a few miles down the road is one of the heartlands of neoliberal capitalism."[20] For Massey, this understanding dispels the idea that the local is either a "hearth of authenticity" or a "victim" to powerful global forces, a binary that can only "lend itself to a politics in which the aim is to defend the local against the global."[21] It permits a switch from "individualized culpability" to "collective responsibility" and advances an "ethics of place, in an actively inventive manner."[22]

Positioned as it is at the nexus of the local and global, theatre might be just the place to experiment with an "ethics of place." But to the extent that it depends deeply on both public and private funding, as it does in Canada, theatre is also suspended between global and world-city agendas. The typically modest scale of theatre production in Canada puts pressure on its artists to adopt a neoliberal language to attract any available levels of funding; at the same time, artists see as clearly as anyone that global cities' dependence on precarious labour fails the very citizens that make those cities vibrant and liveable. The artists celebrated in tourist brochures are the same artists who struggle to sustain a career in the face of rising costs of living. Artists are thus the champions and the discontents of the global city, occupying a position the British playwright Mark Ravenhill lamented in his 2013 address to the Edinburgh Arts Festival, in which he argued that complicity with "creative industry" rhetoric has led artists to create work that is safe and inert.[23] Turning from Florida's global city to Massey's world city requires sufficient artistic freedom to be able to expose uncomfortable truths.

THE MULTICULTURAL POLITICS OF RECOGNITION

The situation described above exposes a gap between the sunny, utopian rhetoric of interculturalism and the continued realities of inequality and precarity. That gap, I want to suggest now, existed also for a previous generation between a new, widely celebrated multicultural Canada and the immense challenges faced by first-generation immigrants. An appreciation of multiculturalism, and particularly its critiques, is important to the direction of my argument in this book.

Official multiculturalism in Canada enshrined in law a respect for the cultural contributions and equal rights of immigrants. Canada's

1.1 Francesco Perilli's *Monument to Multiculturalism* outside Toronto's Union Station. The monument, funded and erected by the city's Italian community and unveiled by mayor Art Eggleton in 1985, is an unambiguous celebration of intercultural harmony.

colonial history, its broken relationship with its indigenous peoples, and its proximity to the United States created a particular need for ideological structures that could manage difference. Canadian multiculturalism was the outcome of a groundswell of cultural nationalism fused with a need to accommodate a large wave of post–Second World War immigrants into the cultural narrative of the country. It was a last-minute modification of what had initially been a bicultural policy reifying the rights of English and French Canadians, broadened to ensure "the recognition and accommodation of cultural diversity."[24] One consequence of multiculturalism, particularly as it was promoted in its early years, was the creation of what the Canadian philosopher Charles Taylor first theorized as a "politics of recognition" within which cultural communities would be encouraged to present themselves to be "recognized" by the dominant culture.[25] Recognition, in sociologist Saskia Sassen's words, was about the "production of presence by those without power."[26]

Although the politics of recognition challenged the homogeneity and colonialism of Canadian culture, it also attracted some fierce discontents. Back in the early 1990s, Neil Bissoondath argued in his influential book *Selling Illusions* that multicultural policy reduced Canadian diversity to fixed cultural positions and traditions to be preserved, which in turn paradoxically erected barriers to integration and inclusion. Developing that argument recently, Sunera Thobani has written that Canadian multiculturalism continues to mark the indigenous and the immigrant "other" either for disappearance or assimilation into an ideologically bicultural nation. That immigrants to Canada could be granted status within the nation was irresistible for them, Thobani writes, but the cost of this acceptance was "increased subservience, across generations, to the grand narrative of national supremacy."[27] These arguments are developed more theoretically in the feminist and queer theorist Sara Ahmed's book *Strange Encounters*, in which Ahmed argues that identifying difference is always and already an act of normalization or domestication. "The production of nation," she writes, "always requires some-body or some-where to not-be in order for it to be."[28] Cultural critic and philosopher Slavoj Žižek similarly describes the position of the "recognizer" in the politics of recognition as an "empty point of universality" that produces a discourse within which "respect of the Other's specificity is the very form of asserting one's own superiority."[29] Through these critiques, multiculturalism sings in harmony with nationalism in a cultural process that hails and guarantees the strangeness of strangers. Also, sociologists and geographers have levelled the criticism against multiculturalism that its logic of fixed cultures is out of step with what the Cambridge social geographer Ash Amin, himself a Ugandan-born British Pakistani, calls "the plural constituency of modern being and belonging."[30] Cultural identity today is usually imagined as something more fluid, extending out through global diasporas or through virtual communities online in sometimes invisible ways. This is the world in which it may make more sense, returning to Chris Rumford's idea, to speak of a condition of "strangeness" rather than of "strangers."[31]

These serious challenges notwithstanding, the multicultural politics of recognition has shaped the way strangers appear in theatre in Canada. As I detail in chapter 2, formal funding structures for the multicultural arts made theatre an important venue for cultural communities to share their experiences and stake their claim on public space. A generation of new playwrights "produced presence" for particular cultural communities in a wave of new plays that spoke openly about experiences of migration, alienation, and prejudice.[32] With the Multicultural Act of 1988, however, the formal funding structures governing how art was stewarded by the state sublimated into a more general logic of multiculturalism and cultural respect for "diversity." In concert with the sociological shifts described above, these changes have created a cultural condition for theatre in Canada within which it is less clear, in a politics of recognition, who is to do the "recognizing." Who are the cultural managers, and where is the cultural centre? Entities that were once the guarantors of stability and cultural coherence, chief among them the nation state and its apparatuses for stewarding culture, have lost some – though certainly not all – control over the inclusion or exclusion of strangers. As Arjun Appadurai has put it, "nation states are not likely to be the long-term arbiters of the relationship between globalization and modernity."[33]

The indeterminacy created in this situation may be something to celebrate, however, in that it points away from cultural politics toward an ethics of difference. For Rustom Bharucha, the most vocal critic of multiculturalism within Theatre Studies, Charles Taylor's schema ultimately became about determining the relative "worth" of cultural communities by adjudicating who was "too different," "not different enough," or "just like us."[34] The way out, in Bharucha's view, is to turn toward an ethics of pluralism, and to turn as well to "emergent cultural practices ... that have resulted in unprecedented interactions with cultural strangers in the public sphere" – in other words, allowing living practices to provoke theory – something I hope to do with the case studies in this book.[35]

The Ghanaian-American philosopher Kwame Appiah also discerns a pivot point between politics and ethics embedded in Taylor's theory. In multiculturalism he finds a "civil apparatus of recognition" that can "ossify the identities that are their object," an effect he dubs the "Medusa Syndrome."[36] Drawing on Taylor's view of culture as constituted in dialogic relation to a social context (rather than as purely a "self"-realization), Appiah writes that, while it may be "too large a claim" to suggest that "the Multicultural chorus must be monological," it is nonetheless true that "the conceptions of collective identity they presuppose are indeed remarkably unsubtle in their understandings of the processes by which identities, both individual and collective, develop."[37] For Appiah, then, a politics of recognition *necessarily* becomes ethical because cultural identification comes with implicit claims for particular, normative views and modes of behaviour that are considered "right" by virtue of being "authentic."[38]

TOWARD A "LIQUID" CANADIAN THEATRE

As much as official multiculturalism was a political project, in this book I take it up as an ethical project. This is to say that, rather than weigh the political or cultural merit of multiculturalism, I am interested in how it continues to shape cultural encounter in the theatre in an increasingly globalized context. Politics, of course, can never be far out of sight. The multicultural politics of recognition and the strain of Western philosophical ethics that I draw on here have in common the project of building utopian communities in which everyone's rights and freedoms are respected. Arguably, a politics of recognition is a prerequisite to an ethics of difference in the sense that an individual or community can only deliberate on ethics if it has the space to do so in the first place. This may be one reason that the global shift in theatre in Canada is taking place at this moment in history and not earlier.

Still, I think it important to avoid an evolutionary narrative that starts with cultural groups being successfully "recognized" and then leads toward their building global ethical relationships. The first problem with such a linear historiography is that politics and ethics are intertwined. I hope to make clear that a politics of recognition and a global ethics both affect the way artists frame their work and how audiences respond to it. Because barriers to equal opportunity persist, many cultural groups remain invested in "producing presence." It is also not easy to know when recognition has been "achieved." Even if written into the highest law of the land, recognition may not be irrevocable, and also may not actually improve people's lives, as demonstrated by the ongoing struggles of Canada's indigenous peoples for equal access to resources, opportunity, and justice. For these reasons, it may be preferable to imagine how ethics leads to politics rather than the other way around. The fact that ethics has emerged as a loud conversation in the Humanities and Social Sciences in recent years may have something to do with a lack of faith in politics as a medium to effectively arbitrate contentious matters of cultural difference and social inequality. In *The Trouble with Strangers*, Terry Eagleton writes: "the idea that the political might pose a challenge to the ethical – that, say, a mode of treating others might be transformed by institutional change – passes largely unregarded."[39] The reverse idea – that ethics may lead to politics – is one response to the dismissive sentiment one sometimes hears, that "theatre is not politics."

I elaborate further on ethics below, but let me say at this point that ethics fuses two ideas: one about determining what actions are "right" in a given context or situation, and the other about the relationship between "self" and "other," or between an "us" and "strangers." Like politics, ethics may also be "public" – although not necessarily. Eagleton, following Lacan, distinguishes an *imaginary* ethics, which includes philosophical, psychoanalytic, and psychological approaches, from a *symbolic* ethics, which sees ethics as public deliberation in an "open field of subjectivity"; the latter includes the arts as one among other possible arenas.[40] In Eagleton's analysis, the moral philosophy of the Enlightenment worked in the realm of the *imaginary* by trying to conceive a utopian moral community as the basis for the modern

European nation-state, a tradition Eagleton says was always "dogged by the hoary old suspicion that altruism might simply be a devious form of egoism."[41] The ethical theories I have been drawn to are primarily the responses to that Western, Enlightenment tradition on the part of theorists with personal and practical experience of living with hybrid cultural identities, and across national borders.[42] Whether these responses have dealt with imaginary or symbolic ethics, they have all highlighted the hidden erasure of the "universal subject." These responses emerged in the wake of the world wars and especially the Holocaust, and have more recently been adapted to thinking about the expanded horizons of a global "moral community."

Prominent among the respondents is the French philosopher Emmanuel Levinas, who argued that Western philosophy's investment in the realization of the perfect "self" fed into an ideological narcissism culminating in the Holocaust, a catastrophe of such magnitude that it required ethics to completely reorient itself around a responsibility to the "other." Many since, such as Enrique Dussel and Peter Singer, have built on Levinas's work to create a new scholarly field of "global ethics," which applies philosophical ethics to the contemporary situation of global inequality. This new theorizing can be understood as an attempt to imagine a more compassionate and sensitive universalism than the one discredited by a series of twentieth-century emancipatory movements. The examples I bring forward in this book should demonstrate how theatre can be an excellent forum in which to think through the horizons of a global ethics.

In addition to being inspired to apply an ethical perspective to the global shift in theatre in Canada by Ahmed's discussion of strangers, I was inspired by a very different thinker, the Polish sociologist Zygmunt Bauman. In dozens of books written over the last three decades, Bauman has examined the consequences of globalization for cultural policy, labour practices, and work habits, the boundary between the public and private, and the relationship of the local to the global. Bauman is best known for his historicization of a "liquid modernity" in the West, which he distinguishes from a preceding "solid" industrial modernity characterized by "vast machinery, huge factories, and massive workforces," and within which "symbolic power [is] defined in terms of volume."[43] For Bauman, the arrival of neoliberal globalization in the form of multinational corporations, highly developed travel and communication systems, and the ascension of the financial and service sectors together represent a fulfilment of Karl Marx's often quoted and prescient phrase, "all that is solid melts into air." As a sociologist, Bauman is especially concerned with a "liquidation of life" observable in "business cycles, employment patterns, family relationships, communal fates, and political horizons."[44] His recurring worries include social alienation (he often uses the term "atomization"), thoughtless consumerism, and spurious notions of "community" which squelch any possibility of ethical encounter. His repeated solution to these problems is to revive deliberative public spaces in which interested citizens can wrest back the control they have surrendered to liquid modernity. It is necessary to "defend the vanishing public realm," he writes, "or rather to refurnish and repopulate the public space fast emptying owing to a desertion on both sides: the exit of the 'interested citizen,' and the escape of real power into the territory which … can only be described as an 'outer space.'"[45]

Bauman has his blind spots – he pays little attention, for example, to gender politics, a shortcoming I address in chapter 3.[46] But it is worth emphasizing that for him the struggle for equality in the public sphere is not a political contest between groups vying for recognition and inclusion but an ethical deliberation around conflicting values. This distinction turns on the notion of "unfixing" cultural identity discussed above. In his book *Community*, Bauman historicizes the politics of recognition as "recognition wars" that "prompt the combatants to absolutize difference … in a string of recognition claims," and suggests that ethics may provide an alternative paradigm:

> If, however, the [recognition wars] are returned to the problematics of social justice where they belong, recognition claims and the policy of recognition become a fertile ground for mutual engagement and meaningful dialogue, which may lead eventually to a new unity – indeed, a widening, rather than a cutting down, of the scope of the "ethical community."[47]

Echoing Appiah, Bauman is careful to say that, while recognition as a human right is the ideal, it need not calcify any state of being. A claim to recognition, rather than demanding "an a priori acceptance of the form of life for which recognition has been or is to be claimed," can instead be "an invitation to dialogue in the course of which the merits and demerits of the difference in question can be discussed."[48] Even with this more ethical discourse decoupled from an absolutist identity politics, however, a question remains about the effect on social justice. Bauman writes: "calls for respect of cultural differences bring little comfort to the many communities that are deprived of the power of independence by virtue of their handicap, and doomed to have their 'open' choices made by other, more substantial powers."[49] The feminist critical theorist Nancy Fraser has likewise observed a "widening gap between the cultural politics of difference and the social politics of equality," and suggests that "justice today requires both recognition and redistribution."[50]

The tension Bauman and Fraser describe between a politics of recognition and an ethics of difference is observable throughout the case studies in this book, and especially in chapters 3 and 4. Theatre can make a contribution to Bauman's deliberative ethical public space, but any contribution is only a *possibility*. Theatre may challenge culture, society, myth, and ideology or it may affirm them. Bauman's provocation to Canadian theatre is to ask whether the staging of strangers provides a chance for meaningful engagement or whether it merely calcifies difference. This question leads him to an additional critique of Bauman's that poses a challenge to Canadian theatre: the "atomization" of politics in "liquid modernity" – what he sees as a devolution of a "capital-p Politics governed by the state into small-scale family and individual 'life politics.'"[51] This is partly a consequence of the fact – explored deeply in his book *Does Ethics Have a Chance in a World of Consumers?* – that postmodern Western society engages its members "in their capacity as consumers rather than producers."[52] Bauman's concern is that the "individual grievances" of these smaller units are non-additive; that is, "they are not amenable to 'summing up' into a 'common cause.'"[53] Worse still, the atomized units may no longer even be able to see that it is *possible* for their efforts to "add up," with the consequence that they are left to seek individualized solutions to what are actually collective, systemic problems. This critique issues a challenge to Canadian theatre on two levels. First, it is arguable that the historical evolution of a set of culturally focused theatre companies (discussed in the following two chapters) has produced such an "atomized" landscape in which collective political solidarity is difficult to achieve (a problem mitigated in recent years by increasing collaboration and resource sharing among these companies). Second, an "atomization" may be at work within the theatre itself in cases in which narratives and characterizations present individualized accommodations to systemic social problems. The telling of personal and often autobiographical stories in Canadian theatre has been a means for the culturally marginalized to be heard and recognized, but might it in other ways have diminished theatre's capacity for "additive" political impact in Bauman's sense?

The institutional and professional precarity of theatre creates an even greater danger of merely affirming difference and precluding the kind of important, ethical interventions of which theatre is capable. The theorists I have mentioned have prompted me to ask whether the kind of difference dealt with in stagings of the stranger is largely superficial. When does theatre fail to deal with cultural difference meaningfully, staging strangers instead in familiar ways, espousing values that few would object to or disagree with (even if they were invited to do so)? Is theatre's consecration of cultural identity antithetical to the possibility of ethically questioning the mechanisms of identity, community, inclusion, exclusion, or encounter – or is this a false dichotomy? When does staging the stranger support a politically and artistically conservative economy of diversity, reproducing difference without difference?

Insofar as these questions call up a critique of an overly "safe" or "affirmational" art, it wouldn't be the first time such a critique was levelled against Canadian theatre. Ric Knowles's critique of poetic naturalism at Toronto's Tarragon Theatre, for instance, has illustrated how Canadian theatre is sometimes guilty of the "deflection of the political by the personal." In this discourse, Knowles writes (in an echo of Bauman's concern about the privatization of politics), change "can only come through individual psychological adjustment to supposed social inevitabilities."[54] As I also do throughout this book, Knowles connects the ethico-political implications back to the poetics of the theatre itself: "political commitment ... exists in order to be resolved in formal cadences rather than to move audiences to action, or even to critical thought."[55] One of my recurring concerns here is also the way in which theatre frames individualized reconciliations as compensations for the deleterious social consequences of globalization.

British sociologist Anthony Giddens more explicitly argues that globalization has produced a world "out of control," a void into which rush compensatory narratives associated with the sacred, domesticity, or, at an extreme, religious or nationalistic brands of fundamentalism and xenophobia.[56] To this list I would add localism, tradition, moral righteousness, and nostalgia, all of which are foundations for what communications scholar Manuel Castells calls "defensive communities," against globalization built around "primary identities."[57] If theatre presents such compensatory narratives uncritically, is it guilty, in Doreen Massey's terms, of playing "victim" to globalization?

Such judgments are highly contextual and difficult to make. Although one sometimes hears Canadian audiences dismissed as being more interested in an entertaining night out than in an experience that questions their values, an audience member who might be thought to be attending the theatre to experience compensatory narratives should not be casually dismissed as apolitical or unwilling to be challenged. The plays and performances I analyze in this book are clear indications that artists and audiences believe that theatre has something of value to contribute to the great geopolitical problems the world faces today. That alone warrants a deep consideration of how the theatre I examine engages audiences and what potential it holds for meaningful ethical encounter. Analyzing how it does so can only be a speculative – and ambivalent – exercise because theatre never succumbs fully to or rejects entirely the ideologies of its day. I am reminded by Michael McKinnie's comment in his excellent materialist analysis of theatre in Toronto that, although "theatre might play a sentimentally affirmative role in a market economy … theatre does not necessarily perform the cognitive work that the mode of production requires for its reproduction."[58] Helen Gilbert and Jacqueline Lo similarly argue that, to whatever extent ideology may condition performance, it "tends to unravel at the point of embodiment" in performance. "Theatre," they write, "engages with how cosmopolitanism is embodied and temporized rather than merely inheriting its sentiment and/or consciousness."[59] In a discussion that makes a virtue of uncertainty, it will be important to appreciate the ways in which theatre manages – sometimes even in spite of itself – to be affirmative and subversive at the same time.

Bauman is sometimes dishearteningly bleak about the possibilities for ethics and, ironically for me, he reserves his keenest pessimism for two important subjects of this book: art and global ethics. But his pessimism is not a devaluation: he values both even as he bemoans their prospects. He never discusses theatre (beyond the occasional theatrical metaphor), but his analysis of cherished Western liberal notions such as "community," "diversity," and "individualism" has everything to do with the ethical relationships theatre is experimenting with in Canada today. I take his urgent call to protect an ethically meaningful public sphere to be also an urgent call for an ethical theatre that, if not fought for, may in a "liquid" modern world find less and less space to thrive.

ON MORALS AND ETHICS

Having set up my discussion as an ethical project, I need to elaborate further on what I take ethics – and then global ethics – to mean in relation to theatre. I am being unabashedly prescriptive here in the sense that I think it worthwhile to understand Canadian theatre in these terms. But my text is also descriptive in the sense that theatre artists have for some time already been working out the ethical practices that address the universalizing, colonialist practices of the past. Two critical paradigms that emerged in the 1980s and 1990s, in fact, each took up this project in their own way: postcolonialism and interculturalism. Postcolonialism pointed to the ways in which artists "spoke back" to colonialism and rejected the authority of the dramatic canon of literature it had produced. Interculturalism focused on the exchange and hybridization of cultures and poetics at the levels of language, narrative, and style. In relation to theatre, each paradigm has argued for responsible processes of engagement across cultural and political borders, and both have been inflected with the language of philosophical ethics.

My argument sits on the shoulders of much older arguments for the role that art can – or should – play in the public sphere. Even in antiquity, Aristotle argued in his *Nicomachean Ethics* that the project of philosophy is not about the good of individuals but about the good of societies. In his *Poetics* he described tragedy as a form of public, ethical encounter that serves society by "clarifying" or "purging" (depending on your translation) its social ills through *katharsis*. The role of art in ethics remained at stake in philosophy down through the Early Modern period, during which theatre became a moral institution implicated in nation building. It was a concern in Enlightenment philosophy from David Hume to Immanuel Kant to Gotthold Lessing, each of whom, in turn, influenced a generation of modern philosophers such as Hannah Arendt, Martha Nussbaum, and Kwame Appiah.

A full accounting for this tradition is neither possible nor necessary here, but from it I have derived a basic distinction that I use in this book: the distinction between the "moral" and the "ethical." In the philosophy of moral aesthetics, "moralism" (occasionally and confusingly also referred to as "ethicism") denotes the view that art should be evaluated for its moral worth, as distinguished from "autonomism," the notion that art should be evaluated purely for formal, aesthetic qualities.[60] While I adopt a broadly "moralist" perspective in these terms, I do not adopt the absolute moralist premise that a work of art may be "morally defective" in ways that must affect its aesthetic evaluation. The moral – less developed in this book than the ethical but important in chapter 4 – is necessarily contextual and can look different with the benefit of hindsight and reflection. For this reason it can be difficult to distinguish it from the deliberative process of ethics. What most cleanly distinguishes the moral from the ethical, however, is that the moral prescribes or anticipates particular values about which, at least from appearances, it has already decided.

Ethics, in my use, divides into two discrete but connected ideas. A *pragmatic ethics* is a debate about right action. It is, as Nicholas Ridout explains in *Theatre and Ethics*, about "character" in the ancient Greek sense of that word, meaning the sum and implication of actions taken (importantly, to be distinguished from the essential and fixed traits implied by the colloquial meaning of "character" in English).[61] Plainly, a pragmatic ethics is about choice – about how and on what grounds choices are made. In addition to this pragmatic ethics of right action, I equally address an *intercultural ethics*, which deals with difference – between the self and the other, the "us" and the stranger – however these are construed. These two ideas thread together in all my analyses below. For those fortunate enough to live in societies in which what constitutes right action is an open question, the theatre is a place where the question can be directly discussed; but the way theatre configures choice is itself revelatory of context-specific values and assumptions. It is one kind of cognitive, affective, social, and aesthetic experience to watch Hamlet struggle about what to do in his famous soliloquy; it is another to be recruited into a performance as a participant – as in the example of *The Stranger* from the Prologue – and be asked to make personal decisions in a public space. Each of these experiences has consequences for how the self is placed in relationship to others.

What makes ethics "meaningful" cannot be "proven" by empirical demonstration. It must, rather, involve a judgment about how meaningfully it stages choices to be made (a pragmatic ethics) and configures an ethical encounter with the other that does not essentialize or reduce the other to the self (an intercultural ethics). A representation may deal with choice and relationships with strangers, but present only obvious choices and deal only in superficial difference – a "soft ethics" that is ethical in appearance but not substance. The line between the moral and ethical may be impossible to discern in some cases, and just barely beneath the surface or readily legible in others. For instance, leaving only a small gap in an otherwise moralistic theatrical representation – the absence, say, of an ephiphanic monologue at the end of a play that sums up a lesson to be learned in the tradition of Early Modern bourgeois tragedies or nineteenth-century stage melodramas – is insufficient alone to make theatre potently ethical.

Two qualities help distinguish the ethical from the moral. The first is that ethics ought to be *difficult*, both in the sense of "difficult choices" and in the sense of a challenging or provocative confrontation with difference. If in a piece of theatre choices are easily made, the encounter with difference lacks friction, and the drama is ultimately benign and involves little disagreement of substance, then we are likely in the territory of the moral. An ethical theatre, by contrast, somehow disturbs or provokes, it chafes against the comfortable, it clears an unfamiliar space into which an audience enters, and it will be stronger for creating these unsettling effects on physical, affective, and intellectual levels. An additional quality of the ethical is the *indeterminacy* of the choices it presents in the theatrical encounter. Whereas the moral is determinate of values, prescribing ways of seeing the world, and explicitly or implicitly guiding the audience in how to feel and think about them, the ethical is indeterminate, presenting choices without anticipating a set of values or providing ready-made solutions. If we already knew "what to do" or how we were to be disposed toward strangers, then there would be no need for ethics. Martha Nussbaum writes that she is attracted to ancient Greek tragedy (as opposed to its philosophy) specifically because of its ethical indeterminacy, what she describes as its "perception of the vulnerability of individual values, such as love, friendship and political commitment."[62] Nussbaum sees ancient Greek dramatic texts "as ethical reflections in their own right … works of distinction to which a culture looked for insight."[63] While philosophy pursues certainties, she argues, tragedy indulges in inconclusive – even impossible – choices.

How does the poetics of theatre, by which I mean its narratives, characters, themes, and modes of engaging with an audience, constitute an ethics of difference in these terms? With which aesthetic and relational strategies does theatre ask its audience to think, feel, or experience? As a medium centred on dramatic tension, argument, and dialogue, theatre should be an ideal ethical art form, but it is just as possible that its tension is trumped up, its dialogue subtly monologic. In his book *The Ethos of Drama*, Robert L. King suggests that theatre sometimes exhibits an implicit singular point of view, a "legible ethos … grounded in the moral character of the play."[64] Citing David Mamet's *Glengarry Glen Ross* as an example, he illustrates how this expectation of a single viewpoint may "flatten" an audience into a position of superiority, distancing it "not in the Brechtian sense of alienation, but in a self-satisfied, unthinking way."[65] This flattening of the audience is possible, too, in theatre that stages strangers. Plays that present themselves as vehicles of social justice and empathy – as conduits through which to know the stranger – may display political or moral commitments that anticipate attitudes in what, at an extreme, can become a "straw" audience. A play that is explicitly or implicitly one-sided in its presentation of a conflict or issue and anticipates a set of known views in its audience would, in my terms, be moral but not ethical. In this book, I read theatrical texts as deliberations on matters that become ethical at the point where they become difficult and indeterminate.

Applying an intercultural ethics to theatre means analyzing how difference is configured at points of encounter. By this I mean something other than the usual postcolonial discussion about cultural appropriation – about who "has the right" to tell whose story. I am interested in what kinds of "seeing," "knowing," and "caring" are implicit in the staging of strangers. Understanding their functioning necessarily involves the audience. In my use in this book, I see the stranger as not inherently or essentially different, but as a figure that produces, or has its difference produced, at the point of encounter with the audience. The stranger contains its audience – or in other words, to be a stranger is to be seen as a stranger. Strangers are not strangers to themselves or in themselves. As Chris Rumford writes, "to be a stranger, in the conventional, Simmelian sense, you have to be seen – and once seen you can be positioned as newcomers, wanderers, foreigners, outsiders."[66] But shaped as theatre is by convention and the specific material conditions of encounter, multiple modes of "seeing" are in play, and "being seen" is more complex than Rumford would have it. Just as strangers appear at the threshold, the ethical also lives at the threshold between stage and audience; and, in my analyses in this book, I oscillate between interpreting theatrical representation – meaning its poetics and theatrical strategies in performance – and studying its relationship with its audience – meaning both the context and the ways it is received or interpreted. Some performances may exhibit a moral poetics by essentializing difference, positioning their audience as "recognizers," and firming up a clear and unquestioned sense of "us" and "them" within the drama and its audience. Other performances may break down categories of difference as a pathway to the ethical.

By emphasizing strangeness rather than strangers, Rumford takes the position that contemporary social life makes it more difficult to determine "who 'we' are, and who 'the other' might be," and theatre as a medium can exploit that ambiguity.[67] What choices does theatre present? Who is invited to choose what, and who is positioned to even extend the invitation? Is the audience invited to watch and judge from a distance, or is it asked to make choices? Who or what is "made strange"? When is seeing strangers *only* seeing strangers, and when does it also imply knowing strangers? Is an audience asked to "recognize" the stranger or asked to extend their empathy or care? Discussing audience in analyses of theatre is notoriously challenging, and I should say that my methodology here did not involve soliciting specific audience members' reactions.[68] I have instead adopted the position of a demanding audience member responding critically to theatre, at points supporting or juxtaposing my interpretations with the written responses of other scholars or critics. I have taken a cue from the American philosopher and playwright Walter Davis, who believes that the responsibility for an ethical theatre falls not just with artists, but with audiences as well: "We will only get the kind of plays we need when we have become the kind of audience who come to the theatre demanding plays that perform such an action within us."[69]

A THEATRE OF GLOBAL ETHICS

I want now to telescope out, and pose these questions within a space of aggressive neoliberal globalization, of huge shifts in labour practices, of deregulated markets that have increased the wealth gap around the world, and of ever-worsening environmental problems that demand a coordinated response. Globally, spaces previously imagined to serve as refuge from the all-pervading logic of globalization – such as the domestic, private sphere of the family – are now permeated by forces originating far beyond the local. In this context, ethical arguments about strangers have become more urgent. The overwhelming scope of that challenge sets stakes for a theatre of global ethics. If there is already reason to think that meaningfully staging strangers is challenging, all the more so for staging distant strangers.

In *The Ethical Project*, the American ethical philosopher Philip Kitcher imagines ethics as an ongoing long-term anthropological human project: "We, collectively, made it up, and have developed, refined and distorted it, generation by generation."[70] In the Enlightenment, a period in which the modern theatre as an element of public culture took shape, philosophers approached the question of moral community with a mind to working up an ideological basis for European nationhood. Several thinkers tried to salvage human goodness from Thomas Hobbes's "man is wolf to man" argument: Adam Smith's *Theory of Moral Sentiments* imagined an "invisible hand" that guides us toward right action in spite of our selfishness;

David Hume's empirical ethicism argued for intrinsic moral motivations moved by passion rather than logical argument; and Immanuel Kant, who learned from and reacted against Hume, built his philosophical system around the problem of how we connect practical first-hand human knowledge to a universally valid grounds for morality. In the global catastrophes of the world wars and the Holocaust, twentieth-century philosophers found cause to return again to first principles. If utopian moral communities had to define themselves against some immoral community of strangers "beyond the pale," the path to a destructive, fascist ideology was short. For Hannah Arendt, the corrective would be a philosophy based in an ethics of compassion; for Emmanuel Levinas, it would be an ethics based in an "infinite responsibility" to the other.

Contemporary efforts to grapple with the relationship to distant strangers have been handled using a set of associated terms such as ethics, empathy, compassion, or care. Whatever the discipline and the organizing concept, the argument that one commonly encounters throughout this body of work is that the human capacity for ethical relationship with distant strangers is *limited*. Some scholars base this argument in evolutionary biology,[71] some in cognitive neuroscience,[72] and others in the anthropological view that human societies evolved only to address problems on the scale of the local.[73] Psychological studies continue to confirm the finding that, as the magnitude of the call to our compassion increases, our perception of our ability to effectively respond to it, and therefore the extent of action we take, decreases,[74] an effect psychologists call "psychic numbing."[75] These discouraging perspectives, however, are mitigated by other research that suggests that our cognitive systems are perfectly capable of overcoming any automatic "shutting down" of inclinations away from empathy or compassion.[76] On balance, scientific perspectives on global ethics confirm the near limits of empathy, but also demonstrate the possibilities of our overcoming them. As the cognitive psychologist Stephen Pinker has argued, the "better angels" of our nature can prevail (and by his dissenting reading of history, they *have* prevailed).[77]

In parallel with these more empirical approaches, contemporary sociologists and philosophers in the academic field of global ethics try to reimagine for our global age the Enlightenment project of the search for moral community. This work tends to agree with the science: while neoliberal globalization is conspiring against a sense of individual agency and ethics, new modes of local and global production, activism, and exchange all reveal possibilities for overcoming the problems. For example, Michael Hardt and Antonio Negri argue that a new postcolonial episteme of "Empire" – not the empire of the colonial period but a new juridical global authority concomitant with twentieth-century globalization – has created an "ethical order" within which choices to intervene in crises or conflicts are justified by appealing to a global notion of moral "right" (by which they mean a Western and especially American sense of what is "right").[78] Following Foucault, Hardt and Negri argue that Empire has sublimated itself from the disciplinary institutions of a prior age such as jails and schools into the fabric of individual subjectivity in the form of a self-legitimizing "biopower."[79] They find ethico-political potential in "a horizon of activities, resistances, wills and desires that refuse the hegemonic order, propose lines of flight and forge alternative constitutive itineraries."[80] It is cause for hope, they observe, that activist efforts today can catapult out of local contexts to secure global attention and action. As another example, the moral philosopher Peter Singer's work builds an ethical argument for extending moral obligations beyond the local – where he thinks our responsibility is experienced absolutely – to the global, where global problems demand global obligations. Singer is discouraged by the gap between the philosophical obligation to distant strangers and the real world failure to realize that obligation (borne out in the first world's paltry commitment to foreign aid as a percentage of GDP). In an unfortunate gesture toward theatre, Singer notes that "a typical affluent country spends more on going to the theatre than many in other countries have to live on for a full year."[81] In other words, there is a disconnect between what people say about global inequality and what they do about it. Whatever the disconnect, the challenge for Singer is urgent: "How well we come through the era of globalization will depend on how we respond ethically to the idea that we live in one world."[82]

Bauman is also interested in global ethics and, like Singer, he too makes an unfortunate gesture toward theatre at the end of *Liquid Modernity* with the idea of "cloakroom communities," a term that uses the temporary gathering of theatre audiences as a metaphor for political organizing that is emotionally charged but short-lived.[83] But if Singer and Bauman were aware of how creatively and passionately theatre artists are attending to global issues and distant strangers, they would not turn to theatre for analogies of complacency. There are reasons why theatre artists would think of theatre as an important medium for staging distant strangers. If, as Bauman suggests, we are to be concerned that globalization has produced a world in which the individual's experience and struggle are private rather than public, in which grievances have become individual rather than collective, then there is potential in the way theatre unfolds the human condition through relationships, in the way it may put a "human face" on otherwise unknowable strangers, or in the way it may engage an audience of active citizens. Theatre is a place in which to take on ethically charged issues in ways that are both galvanizing and personal, private and public, local and global. Theatre can help us determine how to act in a world in which our everyday choices have far-reaching ethical implications.

In this book I examine how the problems these thinkers are grappling with have been playing out in Canadian theatre. I have been propelled by theatre and performance scholar Paul Rae's useful question: "What kinds of stories is the first world telling itself about globalization?" (a question that itself implicates audience in ethics by constructing a questionable first-world "us").[84] In the same spirit of provocation, the French sociologist Luc Boltanski asks: "Why else present a spectacle of suffering human beings to unconcerned people if not to draw their attention to it and so direct them to action?"[85] My analysis does not test how or what is "actionable" in this theatre, in the sense of "impelling to action," but interprets the element's "spectacle" and the means of "drawing attention." I analyze theatrical poetics and strategies for how they configure the audience in an ethics of difference. At points, this analysis implicates the wider conditions of theatrical production (for instance, funding, policy, or access to "mainstream" venues) and reception (for instance, newspaper reviews, scholarship, or audience reportage). I do not propose any practical advice for how to "do" ethical encounter – for there is no "correct" way – but try to provide a language for understanding theatre as an intercultural, intersubjective, ethical encounter. I focus on the plays and their productions, but within this supplemental material also find instructive examples of recognition and misrecognition, acts of making visible and invisible, of values being questioned or assumed.

The book divides into two parts, the first dealing mainly with Georg Simmel's "come today, stay tomorrow" stranger – the immigrant subject who makes a public appearance through theatre[86] – and the second dealing mainly with Chris Rumford's "here today, gone tomorrow" stranger – the distant stranger who appears as a call toward global, ethical relationships.[87] In chapter 2, "Church Basement Globalism," I consider how multiculturalism configured the work of Toronto's nonprofessional culturally focused theatre groups.[88] Although many of these theatres have a long history and still exist today, they have been largely dismissed by critics and scholars for lacking artistic merit or for being inclined toward nostalgia. I argue, however, that such judgments are themselves a product of multiculturalism, within which the stranger could only be recognized as a decontextualized and folkloric other. The chapter uses the example of Toronto's half-century-old Czech and Slovak Nové divadlo (New Theatre) to expose how multiculturalism has obscured a different *global* axis of recognition.

Chapter 2, "Domesticating the Stranger," explores how Simmel's "here today, stay tomorrow" stranger has appeared in the professional culturally focused theatre. This theatre differed from church basement globalism in that it produced new original Canadian plays from first- or second-generation Canadians, opening a space to tell widely experienced stories of displacement and marginalization. The chapter zeroes in on a popular narrative in this theatre: the "generational family drama" that depicts the second-generation immigrant subject's divided obligations and conflicted identity. I use examples of this narrative that span two decades – Betty Quan's *Mother Tongue,* Catherine Hernandez's *Singkil*, and Ins Choi's *Kim's Convenience* – to consider the ethical implications of constructing the domestic sphere as a refuge from the deprivations of globalized modernity. I argue that, while this theatre has to a large extent overcome the folklorizing multicultural narrative, it may in some cases have also "domesticated" the stranger by bypassing ethical questions about what forces may keep strangers "at the threshold."

The fourth chapter, "A New Melodrama of Globalization," turns to the "here today, gone tomorrow" stranger to argue that melodrama is the primary mode of the distant stranger's appearance on Canadian stages today. Melodrama, a popular form of entertainment in the nineteenth century, responded to the social upheavals of the Industrial Revolution and affirmed certain social values in opposition to a newly aggressive capitalism. The new melodramas of globalization on the Canadian stage respond in like manner to neoliberal globalization, calling attention to those it has poorly served and proposing an ethical relationship to distant strangers. This new melodrama shares many features with its antecedents, such as the pursuit of "moral legibility" in an ethically fraught world, the rendering of overwhelming social problems into personal terms, and the protection of "spaces of innocence."[89] Two previously mentioned plays, both produced or co-produced by Cahoots' Theatre Company, exhibit all of these features: Ahmed Ghazali's *The Sheep and the Whale* and Matthew MacKenzie's *SIA*. These plays feature a new melodramatic trope: a crusading "white knight" on a quest to help distant strangers, a story seemingly intent on galvanizing moral conviction in its audience.

To look at examples of theatre pursuing supposedly more "active" relationships between stage and audience, my last chapter, "Making Strange: The 'Active' Audience," considers the ethical potential of more participatory, immersive, or relational forms of theatre. The first example in the chapter, It's a Freedom Thing Theatre's site-specific performance *Nightmare/Dream*, conceived and directed by Ugandan and Kenyan Canadian theatre artist Mumbi Tindyebwa Otu, provides a chance to think about how the "generational family drama" of chapter 2 can be realized through different aesthetics and ways of engaging the audience. The second example, the indigenous theatre group Debajehmujig Storytellers' international theatre project *The Global Savages*, presents other possibilities for ethics by toying with the idea of the fetishized stranger and relating to its audience in a uniquely layered and sustained way. Both examples demonstrate the potential for theatre to create a more indeterminate ethical relationship with audiences. In my Epilogue, "Stranger Danger," I briefly consider the stranger as a contemporary object of fear in the context of a renewed xenophobia in the West, and suggest what have for me been the most valuable insights of this project.

In all the discussions that follow my hope is to call attention to the both exciting and concerning ways that staging strangers in contemporary theatre in Canada is making a world of difference. I want to argue for a theatre that stages the stranger as a figure who focuses and amplifies a productive ethical compassion for and obligation to strangers. Beyond the stimulation that I hope the book offers to discussions of theatre in Canada, my hope is that it also contributes to a larger argument for theatre as a vital cultural arena, possessed of unique assets for posing the challenging, ethical questions that need to be asked in a complex, globalized world. I hope to help theatre to "make a world of difference" in that other sense of the phrase: for it to be relevant, impactful, and implicated in the critical ethical questions of the moment.

2

Church Basement Globalism

How does multiculturalism reinvent "the nation" over the bodies of strangers? How does the act of "welcoming the stranger" serve to constitute the nation? How is the "we" of the nation affirmed through the difference of the "stranger cultures," rather than against it?

Sara Ahmed, *Strange Encounters*[1]

Alan Filewod in 1989 noted the tendency to explain Canadian culture "as something that grows from colonial infantilism to an undefined 'world-class' maturity."[2] The midway point of this imagined "maturation story," I would suggest, took place in the 1970s and '80s when new cultural voices diversified the country's dominant Anglo and Franco cultures. A problem with this story – that is, in addition to its neglect of Canada's indigenous peoples – is its inattention to the contribution of earlier waves of immigrants to Canada. In the realm of theatre, communities of immigrants established theatre groups that sustained the traditions of their home cultures and ameliorated the isolation of exile. These nonprofessional groups comprised strangers of Georg Simmel's "come today, stay tomorrow" type,[3] who staged theatre in their own language primarily in and for their own cultural communities. The tradeoff for their speaking "in" their communities and performing beyond the usual spaces of the professional arts in ethnic halls or church basements, was that such groups situated themselves beyond any cultural process of "recognition" by the wider culture.[4] What the "maturation story" has right is that these groups did briefly perform "out" of their communities in the 1970s and '80s. In government-funded multicultural theatre festivals, they performed plays of their respective national repertoires for audiences from within and beyond their cultural communities. Festivals afforded opportunities to share their culture with wider audiences but, given that groups still usually performed in their own language, audiences weren't always able to understand what they saw. As a result, the theatre that these groups produced came to be seen as folkloric, sentimental, and artistically unremarkable, doubly marginalized for being both amateur and foreign. Re-inventing the nation "over the bodies of strangers," as Ahmed writes, the activities of these groups buttressed multicultural Canada. At that cultural moment multicultural theatre positioned the dominant Canadian culture as warden of the nation's hospitality, in a position to "welcome the stranger" – the strangers in this case being mainly first-generation immigrants.[5]

In this chapter, after first situating nonprofessional culturally focused theatre within Canadian multiculturalism, I will be more precise about how the stranger is staged within this tradition by zeroing in on Toronto's Czech and Slovak theatre group Nové divadlo (Czech for "New Theatre"), which formed almost fifty years ago and is still active today. I choose Nové divadlo because of my background with the Czech Republic; I worked on a partly Czech-based theatre project between 1999 and 2006, lived in Brno, Czech Republic, in 2007, and have studied the Czech language. That perspective enables me to see how the discourse and structures of multiculturalism occluded what I will call Nové divadlo's "church basement globalism" – its exchange with Czech and Slovak professional artists, its intermixing of aesthetics and styles through diasporic circuits, and even its staging of material that was banned at "home." I don't discuss Nové divadlo's productions in detail, but show how they appeared to the dominant culture through multicultural theatre festivals. It is instructive to look at how one critic in particular responded to Nové divadlo – Herbert Whittaker, whom Ronald Bryden exalted in the 1970s as "*the* principal witness to the most important decades of Canada's theatre history … the years in which theatre in Canada evolved into the Canadian theatre."[6] Whittaker's commentary, though understandable within the cultural context and the tradition of Canadian theatre criticism of its time, legitimized a particular way of seeing – if not especially knowing – strangers. Nové divadlo's encounters with the dominant culture reveal the biases of multiculturalism and a need to tilt the axis of "recognition" toward the global.

THEATRE IN CHURCH BASEMENTS

Canada's official policy of multiculturalism created neither difference nor the need to deal with it. What it did was to organize both established and nascent communities within a liberal political agenda. Jacqueline Lo and Helen Gilbert distinguish a "small-m multiculturalism" a "community generated consciousness," from a "big-M Multiculturalism," an official policy "that has played a significant role in nation building since the 1970s."[7] Using their distinction, Canada was multicultural long before it was officially "Multicultural" on account of three major waves of immigration, each with a distinct character: one in the early twentieth century, another following the Second World War, and a third spread out over the 1990s and 2000s.

The first two waves had a dramatic impact on the cultural makeup of the country. The sudden influx of immigrants at the turn of the nineteenth century raised the percentage of foreign-born Canadians to nearly 25 percent, a ratio the country has not exhibited since.[8] The crest of this wave of immigration came in the closing years of the nineteenth century when then Prime Minister Laurier and Minister of the Interior Clifford Sifton aggressively campaigned to settle the Prairies with European immigrants. As Zygmunt Bauman writes in his own periodization of immigration into three phases, this first phase can be seen as "partly exportation and partly eviction of up to 60 million people ... to 'empty lands' (read: lands whose native population could be struck off the 'modernized' calculations)."[9] The second wave of immigrants arrived in the sobering aftermath of the Second World War, when a new spirit of tolerance was in the air: the Canadian Citizenship Act was passed to redress the racist and xenophobic policies of the 1906 and 1919 immigration acts; Ontario passed a discrimination act that criminalized racial and religious discrimination; and a 1923 act that forbade Chinese immigration was repealed in 1947, ending the so-called "exclusionary era." At mid-century, Canada was still predominantly European, with English and French groups followed by a long list of other immigrant groups from Europe. The second wave of immigration subsided in the 1970s, gradually giving way to a third wave that took hold in the 1990s when the Canadian government – cognizant of its aging population and declining birth rates, and of a shortage of labour in the increasingly important service industry – opened the doors to other parts of the world. The doors have been open since, producing a stretched out period of high, constant immigration over three decades. This wave of immigrants has differed from the earlier ones, partly on account of the criteria for admission shifting from being based on origin to being based on points awarded for education, age, language fluency, and employability (with special consideration given to refugees or those immigrating to join family). The third wave saw higher numbers of immigrants from South Asia, the Middle East, Latin America, and Africa. Toronto began to emerge as a preferred destination, such that between 2001 and 2006 the city accepted about a quarter of the country's immigrants,[10] and in some suburban areas of Toronto, two-thirds of the newcomers have been Asian.[11]

For all these immigrants the multicultural reality has not always looked like the Multicultural dream. Ethnic and religious tensions have at times transferred from elsewhere and mixed with new ones fuelled by the social and economic anxieties of war, economic depression or recession, and barriers to opportunity. Cramming together the world's displaced and economically precarious migrants in the first two waves was a massive social experiment, and unprepared Canadian governments ham-fistedly created and revised policies that denied immigrants equivalent status and citizenship. The British Columbian Provincial Elections Act of 1895, for example, stipulated that "[no] Chinaman, Japanese or Indian shall have his name placed on the Register of Voters of any Electoral District, or be entitled to vote at any election."[12] Throughout the twentieth century, the Chinese have been scapegoats for multiple social ills. In 1907, for example, when the Asiatic League in Victoria tried to stage a parade, the scene turned into a riot, with people displaying racist banners such as "White Canada – patronize your own race and Canada."[13] The revised Immigration Act of 1919 was perhaps a nadir; the government refused entry not only to citizens of all its enemy countries from the war, but also to the disabled and to several religious and ethnic communities. In the infamous *Komagata Maru* incident in 1914, a boatload of almost four hundred immigrants was sent back to India after being detained for weeks in Vancouver's Burrard Inlet. When tough economic times struck in 1931, an Order in Council halted nearly all immigration save for the wealthiest applicants. There was evidence of widespread anti-Semitism in the early century as well. In 1933 a riot broke out in Toronto's Christie Pits Park when a Nazi group unfurled a swastika flag in front of a mostly Jewish softball team playing in the park. Nobody was charged. In Canada, strangers have had plenty of reason to feel "not welcome."

No wonder, then, that immigrants to Canada were at certain times reluctant to perform their culture out to the broader Canadian public. But when they organized within their cultural communities across the country, they invariably mixed musical, dance, and theatrical performances into their activities in legion halls, public libraries, and church basements. In the early twentieth century, such theatre groups mainly produced folk plays from the rural parts of Europe from which that generation of farmer-immigrants had come. In some cases the groups comprised a loose collection of enthusiasts; in others, they were well organized and networked in regional chapters. Associations of Armenians, Macedonians, Serbs and Croats, for instance, each put on plays in Toronto and across Southern Ontario throughout the interwar period.[14] The Ukrainian community stood out for its size and activity. There were more than 300,000 Ukrainians in Canada by the Second World War (a number surpassed only by those of British, French, or German origin[15]), and their theatre output was significant; one amateur historian notes that in the 1920s and '30s, "every local Ukrainian hall and parish had a drama group of its own,"[16] and that by 1941, "Ukrainian Canadians had written and produced at least 100 original plays."[17]

The second wave of immigration to Canada led to the formalization of the more ad-hoc theatre groups into more structured, sustained, and regularly producing organizations. It is difficult to say how many of these companies popped up across the country in the 1950s and '60s, but Toronto alone saw the appearance of the Italian Piccolo Teatro (1949), the Lithuanian drama group Seitynas (1950) and its Hamilton counterpart Aukuras (1950), the Latvian D.V. Theatre Company (1951), the Czechoslovak Theatre Group (1951, a precursor to "Nové divadlo"), the Polish literary and theatre club Dragon's Den, or "Smocza Jama" (1951), the Estonian National Theatre (1955), the Ukrainian Dramatic Ensemble "Zahrava" (1957), and the Hungarian Art Theatre (1958), all of which joined earlier organizations such as the Finnish Social Club (1932), the Chinese United Dramatic Society (1933) and the Ship Toy Yuen Dramatic Society (1935).[18]

Despite the fact that the collective output of these groups was remarkable, theatre critics from mainstream newspapers rarely mentioned them. That isn't surprising, given that most of their activity took place in a foreign language. Filling the gap were "ethnic" newspapers, more than five hundred of which are estimated to have existed in Ontario alone over the last century, publishing in forty different languages.[19] But the fact that *Globe and Mail* theatre critic Herbert Whittaker could write in 1972 that "up until a few years ago, it was a notable fact that new arrivals to Toronto from other lands rarely included theatre-goers," was an indication of how willfully unaware some publics were to the large output these groups have had since the nineteenth century.[20] Robert F. Harney, founder of the Multicultural History Society of Ontario, was one of the few people to ever devote scholarly attention to their activities. "It is startling," he wrote in 1983, "to discover how little serious study has been given to the intense and vibrant tradition of live ethno-cultural theatre, which has been with us since the turn of the century and the age of mass immigration."[21] For the society's publication *Polyphony*, Harney curated what remains the only collection of articles looking at this phenomenon from a broad perspective. What other commentary has appeared about the "immigrant" theatre – at least up until very recently, when amateur theatre practices have been looked at anew by theatre historians – dismisses it as nostalgic and parochial. It is as though the immigrant theatre fulfilled the hoped-for multicultural dream not because of their choices of repertoire or approach but just by virtue of their existence. Jacqueline Lo and Helen Gilbert, who identify this type of theatre as "ghetto theatre," describe it this way:

> Ghetto theatre tends to be monocultural; it is staged for and by a specific ethnic community and is usually communicated in the language/s of that community. The political efficacy of this type of multicultural intervention is arguably limited since the perfor-

> mances are largely "in-house" and tend to focus on narratives about origins and loss. Much ghetto theatre is infused with a nostalgic privileging of the homeland (real or imagined) as seen from a diasporic perspective, with the result that more radical cross-cultural negotiations are muted.[22]

The language of the passage – "ghetto" and "monocultural" – rhetorically marginalizes these theatre groups, adopting the view that they are culturally affirmational and unremarkable. Implicit in the passage too is a valuation of multicultural theatre for its "political efficacy." The implication that the insularity of "church basement theatre" must make it politically inert, however, suggests that the political is being specifically understood to denote a minoritized culture's intervention in a wider public; it is, in other words, the politics of recognition. In addition to their "ghetto theatre" being spatially marginalized, it is also suspended in time; immigrant communities are aligned with the past, with the loss of their origins, nostalgic for "getting back home." This gesture plucks strangers out of time and place and denies their activities any socio-political relevance. Ric Knowles suggests a different framing of the activities of these immigrant groups in his book *Theatre and Interculturalism*. Although Knowles also notes their "residual tendency to promote compensatory nostalgias," he qualifies the judgment with the suggestion that immigrant theatre might also be the source of a "productive internationalization of Canadian Multiculturalism."[23] Nonprofessional groups, he intimates, might contribute something other than folklore to Canada, although he still conscripts them into an ideological fulfillment of multiculturalism.

The policy of multiculturalism, however, may have been as responsible for these groups' momentary visibility to the dominant culture as it has been for their usual invisibility. As a policy and a cultural ethos, multiculturalism has arguably had the effect of keeping strangers, in this case mainly first-generation immigrants, at the threshold of Canadian culture – neither fully "othering" nor welcoming them. All the while, however, these nonprofessional culturally focused groups have not only been seeking political recognition within Canadian multiculturalism but, at least in some cases, also seeking recognition across a diasporic circuit within their respective home contexts. Robin C.

Whittaker, a historian of Canadian nonprofessional theatre, remarks on the same possibility: "nonprofessionalized theatre practices … are rarely contextualized beyond the local community [and] are normally viewed without geographically ranging significance."[24] A more acute attention to the church basement globalism of these groups reveals the selective way in which multiculturalism stages strangers. It permits a reframing of Toronto not as "the most multicultural city in the world," but as one node in an interwoven network of cultural diasporas.

CZECH-CANADIAN THEATRE

A rich example of church basement globalism is the theatre produced over the last century by the Czech and Slovak Canadian community.[25] Czechs have a long history in Canada, symbolized perhaps by "Prince Rupert of the Rhine," a Prague-born Bohemian prince who in the seventeenth century was granted Royal charter to form the Hudson's Bay Company in "Rupert's Land." The Czechs first came in large numbers as a result of Sifton's policy to populate the West, with cultural enclaves appearing first in Kolin, Saskatchewan, and Michel, British Columbia. Early Czech immigrants brought to Canada the energy of the Czech National Revival (*národní obrození*), a nineteenth-century popular nationalist movement that liberated the country from three centuries of Austro-Hungarian rule, a crowning achievement of which was the building, and the rebuilding following a fire, of the National Theatre in Prague entirely from funds raised by the people.[26] Czech immigrants quickly organized in Canada. Josef Čermák, a longtime member of the Czech nonprofessional theatre community in Toronto, notes that the Czechoslovak Benevolent Association, which formed in 1913, had thirty branches across the country a decade later.[27] Two later pulses of immigration to Canada from the region took place in 1948 and 1968, and comprised refugees fleeing German, and then Soviet, annexations.[28] Up until the Second World War, the Czech community in Toronto met at Masaryk Hall on Queen Street (still serving today as a community centre in the city's Parkdale neighbourhood), but in 1948 it purchased a sixty-four-acre plot of farmland in Scarborough where it would build Toronto's home for the Czech and Slovak community, the Masaryk Memorial Institute. Referred to as "Masaryktown" within the community, the cultural and educational centre remains a busy hub of activity today, having in part a mandate to "disseminate the best in Canadian and Czechoslovak literature and art."[29]

The Czechs brought to Canada the tradition known in Czech as *ochotnícke divadlo*, or "goodwill theatre." Čermák notes performances of Czech plays and folk dances in Canada going back as far as 1933 (though no doubt they were happening for decades earlier as well). The arrival of thousands of Czechs to Toronto in 1948 catalyzed the creation of a new regularly producing organization calling itself the Czechoslovak Theatre Group.[30] Newcomers joined and directed productions: Zdeněk Dostál directed *Maryša* and *Princezna Pampeliška* (*Princess Dandelion*), Jindra Dozer directed *Tři a jeden* (*Three and One*), and Karel Čapek's *R.U.R.* (the play that introduced the word "robot," which means "worker" in Czech, to the English language). František Sobotka and Ruza Karycova-Haisová were the primary movers in the community during the 1950s, managing a steady stream of productions.

The makeup of the Czech-Canadian community shifted dramatically in 1968 as a result of the invasion of Prague by the Warsaw Pact countries (called the *Pražské jaro* or "Prague Spring").[31] Many Czechs fled the country as fast as they could, and large groups eventually found their way to Toronto and Vancouver.[32] Those they left behind would have to endure a bleak period of Soviet "normalization" during which the theatre would be censored and political dissent silenced. The 1968 wave of Czechs and Slovaks were a different group than those who had come before, mainly comprising young professionals, "college graduates, doctors, engineers, lawyers, and also actors, writers, musicians and filmmakers."[33] They had a comparatively easier time adjusting than many other immigrant groups, though challenges remained.[34] Artists arriving in Canada from Europe, some with conservatory training and impressive resumés, still found themselves shut out of a professionalizing arts industry in Canada.

Such was largely the case for Adolf Toman, born during the Second World War in Pardubice and raised in nearby Nymburk. Toman was educated in the early 1960s in Prague's Academy for the Performing Arts (DAMU) – the larger of the Czech Republic's two conservatory theatre schools then as now – where he had trained among a generation of postwar artists who were reviving the Czech avant-garde of the 1920s and '30s.[35] Fresh out of theatre school, Toman had a promising career; but it collided with the Prague Spring, and he fled, initially to France as many other Czechs did at the time, and from there to Canada. Though he came to Toronto because, as he put it, "he wanted to see Niagara Falls,"[36] it proved fertile ground. In his two productive decades in the city, Toman sustained two projects in parallel: the Limelight Dinner Theatre and Nové divadlo. The Limelight was a successful semi-professional operation that produced mainly canonical Western plays and popular American musicals in English for a broad audience (initially at the Colonnade Theatre on Bloor Street and after 1979 at an uptown location still operating today as the Mysteriously Yours Dinner Theatre). For years at the Limelight, Toman would produce popular musicals accompanied by meals and drinks at intermission. These shows were low-budget, ramshackle adaptations, and production values often strained the sympathies of the critics who deigned to attend. Of one production at the Limelight, Ray Conlogue wrote in the *Star*: "it produces these sprawling old hits on a tiny stage with a tinier budget. There's no doubt the single set which lamely tries to pretend it is different locations by having small identifying slides projected above its paper-mache fireplace is tacky, and that the 13 performers ... are quite a ways this side of Broadway slick."[37]

As unpolished as the Limelight's musicals may have been, Conlogue's response lacked a full context for what Toman was doing. In 1960s Czechoslovakia, where Toman came of age, improvisatory cabaret adaptations of popular and literary stories had become common in the "club" or "studio" theatres in venues such as Studio Ypsilon and Divadlo na zábradlí in Prague or Husa na provázku in Brno. After the Prague Spring, this popular and ostensibly "safe" source material, improvised upon by skilled actors in performance, could evade censorship to pass surreptitious political comment on the Soviet regime.[38] Critics in Canada could not have been expected to be aware of an alternative movement in a closed Communist country halfway around the globe, but this small misrecognition of Toman's work nonetheless foreshadowed a situation that would develop around his second project, the one that would permit him to form a conduit between Toronto and Prague in an expression of "church basement globalism."

Immediately implicating himself on his arrival in Toronto into its large Czech and Slovak expat community, Toman and a group of like-minded theatre enthusiasts got together in December 1969 to revive and rebrand the stagnant Czechoslovak Theatre Group into the Czech and Slovak New Theatre, or Nové divadlo. The group would perform in the Limelight on Sundays, but also in the lobby of Masaryktown in Scarborough, and later in other venues such as the St Lawrence Theatre, Poor Alex, Harbourfront Theatre, Mimico High School Theatre, Adelaide Court, and the Hart House and Robert Gill theatres at the University of Toronto. Operating continuously since it was formed, Nové divadlo has now produced over 150 productions – an impressive output for a group dependent almost entirely on volunteers.

NOVÉ DIVADLO AT THE MULTICULTURAL THEATRE FESTIVALS

Nové divadlo's reception in the years following its formation illustrates one specific way in which multiculturalism stages strangers. In my first chapter I suggested that a multicultural politics of recognition in Canada may have, in Sunera Thobani's words, marked immigrant strangers "either for disappearance or assimilation into an ideologically bicultural nation."[39] In the 1970s and '80s, groups such as Nové divadlo were regarded by the wider culture in a way that both recognized their presence and guaranteed their strangeness.

It turned out that Toman had formed Nové divadlo at an auspicious moment in the development of nonprofessional culturally focused theatres in Canada. When Toman arrived in Canada in the late 1960s, the political establishment of the country was under pressure to respond to fundamental changes to the country's demographics. As Yasmeen Abu-Laban and Christina Gabriel detail in their book *Selling Diversity,* the postwar wave of immigrants had produced such public "presence" that the then recently established Royal Commission on Bilingualism and Biculturalism had to evolve from a policy about French and English Canada into a policy of multiculturalism, which Pierre Trudeau's government would make official in 1971. A year later Trudeau appointed a minister of state for multiculturalism tasked to fit the existing, grassroots ecology of ad-hoc organizations to the new multicultural brand. The government enlisted the aid of the organizations themselves. At the first Canadian conference on multiculturalism in October 1973, what was then called the Secretary of State Department brought together 250 delegates from cultural communities across the country to discuss how their activities should be funded. One outcome was discrete funding for the "Multicultural Arts" to be distributed by the "Multiculturalism Directorate," a sub-office of the secretary of state. Straight away, the new directorate organized the array of nonprofessional, culturally focused theatre companies into provincial Multicultural Theatre Associations (MTAs). From 1975 on these would be networked together within a National Multicultural Theatre Association (NMTA), which acted "as a liaison between provincial associations, disseminating ideas and news, promoting the exchange of productions, personnel and material, and establishing a national publication."[40] After 1979 the NMTA would represent the interests of Canadian nonprofessional theatre alongside provincial organizations such as Theatre Ontario and Theatre Alberta (established in 1971 and 1981 respectively and both still in operation).[41] For the government, the benefits of this structure were both pragmatic and political: they needed a mechanism to deliver funding to cultural groups that were too numerous and casually organized to manage individually; and successive Liberal governments between 1963 and 1979 were also casting about for support from new blocks of immigrant voters. As Carol Off wrote cynically of the funding of the Multicultural Arts in 1988, "the government has always eagerly funded such folk arts in exchange for healthy rounds of applause and hopefully healthy turn-outs at the ballot box."[42] By the end of the 1980s all ten provinces had either an MTA or another similar organization embracing multiculturalism.[43]

The theatre groups embraced the arrival of the MTAs. For one thing, the MTAs offered an opportunity to network with other itinerant cultural groups whose activities around the city had been as unseen to one another as they had been to the dominant culture. They also presented an opportunity to share audiences. The whole raison d'être of the MTAs was to organize annual multicultural provincial theatre festivals and a national festival, to be held in a different Canadian city each year. For two decades, the national festival was the only national festival of Canadian theatre at all, filling a void left by the demise of the long-running Dominion Drama Festival. Among the six original members of the Ontario Multicultural Theatre Association, Nové divadlo performed shows regularly at its annual festival, and Toman served as the association's artistic director in 1977. Proud of its work, Nové divadlo fully seized the moment to share the Czech cultural repertoire through the festivals. For the first time since the group had been formed, its work could be seen by wider audiences and critics, placing it in a new position between Czech cultural traditions and the rapidly changing theatre industry in Canada.

If it was a kind of victory for these strangers at the threshold to be seen, it would unfortunately not mean that they would be well known. Predictably, the MTAs had made no provision for how audiences or critics beyond these cultural communities were to understand and interpret their work. Herbert Whittaker, theatre critic for the *Globe and Mail* from 1949 to 1975, nonetheless demonstrated an admirable goodwill and effort. He took a special interest in the Czechs. Take, for instance, his 1969 review of George Luscombe's *Good Soldier Švejk* at Toronto Workshop Productions, in which he wrote, "the Czech stage has a reputation for gay experimentation and witty staging,"[44] or his kind words for a student production of Václav Havel's breakout play *Memorandum* at Trinity College in 1969,[45] or his praise in 1978 for Czech-Canadian Jan Rubeš (husband of Susan Douglas Rubeš, founder of Toronto's Young People's Theatre) for bringing the renowned – if by that time less critically celebrated – Czech theatre Laterna Magika to Toronto.[46] In Whittaker's review of the first Multicultural Theatre Festival in 1972, he mentioned Nové divadlo first, calling their production of Fráňa Šrámek's 1915 play *Summer* a "bright new hope," even though he flagged the play's nostalgia by calling it a "sentimental romance" (not an unfair criticism; the wordy, lyrical play is rarely produced and has little conflict – a puzzling choice for the company's first entry in the festival).[47] He doled out similarly qualified praise for their contribution to the festival the next year, František Hrubín's *Oldřich and Božena, or A Bloody Conspiracy in Bohemia,* a play depicting an obscure episode in medieval Czech history in which a Bohemian prince weds a foreign peasant girl and complicates plans for royal succession. Back home, Hrubín's play had, like many others, used allegory to pass political comment. Written and rehearsed in the lead up to the Prague Spring and performed in its wake, it was a thinly veiled exploration of the playwright's own turbulent time, written, in Hrubín's own words, "to consider the key to human history as a question mark rather than a seemingly precise record or cipher that is too self-assured."[48] Lacking that context for the play and thwarted by the language barrier, Whittaker could write only that, "for non-Czechs, the high rhetoric was baffling, but Toman's skill in handling fights and deaths balanced the long confrontations."[49]

Whatever the MTAs' pretentions toward multicultural inclusivity, the exposure they offered gave groups such as Nové divadlo little more than a modest and tentative purchase on public attention beyond their community. The sun began to set on the MTAs in the early 1990s as more people saw funding for the multicultural arts as the well-meaning but counterproductive strategy that it was. Concern had been expressed even back at the 1973 multiculturalism conference, when Hania Federowicz, then president of the Polish theatre group Arabeska, declared that she "didn't want to be paid for being ethnic" but preferred to compete with other Canadian artists "on the basis of its art."[50] By the 1990s, a neo-conservative xenophobia produced a new pitched battle over identity politics, cultural inclusion, and equal opportunity. When, for example, in November 1990, the then acting Manitoba minister of culture and heritage, Harold Neufeld, stated that he was "against Multiculturalism because it meant WASPs [were] paying for everyone else's culture," the Manitoba Association for Rights and Liberties pointed out that the "cultures" of the CBC and the Manitoba Theatre Centre were also very well funded.[51] Of the controversy, John Dafoe asked in the *Globe and Mail* whether those mainstream institutions were not themselves deeply multicultural, and whether it wasn't itself "distorted and exclusionary" to think that Western culture did not belong to all Canadians.[52] Neil Bissoondath's *Selling Illusions* soon added further support to the argument that multiculturalism was based on a preservationist policy that erected barriers to inclusion. Though multiculturalism had enabled some material gains for cultural minorities – one of which was the trend toward professionalization in the theatre discussed in the following chapter – it was besieged as a cultural policy. Multiculturalism's sublimation into the 1988 Multiculturalism Act represented a move away from constructing any culture as *not* multicultural, a situation that had affirmed the authority of the dominant culture.

My key interest here is in what kind of appearance or disappearance multiculturalism afforded strangers. For Nové divadlo and the dozens of other similar groups who would participate in the MTAFs in the 1970s and 80s, multiculturalism brought one kind of recognition and approval by the official structures. Members of Nové divadlo rightly saw it as a victory to have appeared in a festival on a major Toronto stage such as the St Lawrence Centre, where their otherwise overlooked activities would be written about by a mainstream critic such as Whittaker. But this was a weak form of recognition that could make no claim on any wider cultural impact, much less have any concrete material implication. Blaik Kirby's comment in the *Globe* in 1972, that "the [MTA] Festival can deservedly boast that it has brought Toronto's ethnic performers into the mainstream" vastly overestimated the impact these appearances afforded these cultural groups.[53] Their productions at the festivals would only be regarded at their surfaces and never be contextualized in relation to foreign traditions. Of course this was an inevitable consequence of the plays' being performed in their own language, and it was a bit naïve to suggest, as Whittaker did at the time, that the festivals would "awaken interest in the study of languages."[54] It was a lot to expect English-speaking audiences and critics to attend – and understand – performances in foreign languages. Whittaker's unsatisfying solution was to write through the language barrier as if it wasn't there, passing judgment on whatever theatrical elements were legible to him. He established the pattern in a 1973 visit to Prague, when, presumably out of a wish to see work with which he was familiar, he saw productions of Chekhov and Shakespeare, but only one Czech play, Karel Čapek's *The Robber*, at Divadlo na vinohradech. Whittaker praised Josef Svoboda's scenography for the production – a more legible element of the performance for him – and a single comment about his "disappointment" that the poetic pleasures of the play's text were "denied" him is notable for being the only mention Whittaker makes, seeing a play performed in Czech either in Prague or in Canada, of the language barrier.

I don't mean to make a straw man of Whittaker, who is singularly impressive among theatre critics at the time for how seriously he took Adolf Toman, Nové divadlo, and the nonprofessional culturally focused theatre generally.[55] Being from Montreal, having worked in both English Canada and Quebec, and having travelled extensively, Whittaker was wise to the limits of his intercultural understanding. But it is *because* Whittaker paid attention to the group that his reviews most clearly reveal a failure not in him, but in the way multiculturalism failed to create the meaningful, ethical encounter for which I argued in the previous chapter. Audiences to the MTAFs could not comprehend across the language barriers either, and many came only to see plays of their own cultural community. Blaik Kirby observed of the first MTAF in Toronto in 1972 that "comparatively few 'Canadians' attended," and that "most of the patrons were immigrants, though there was some mixing among groups"[56] – a statement with the unfortunate implication that immigrants were not "Canadians" that echoes Georg Simmel's idea of the stranger as "no owner of soil." Kirby then retreated, as Whittaker did, into the extra-linguistic: "No doubt music helps to bridge the language gap."[57]

Such comments hint at the fact that the well-intentioned multiculturalism surrounding the MTAFs was designed to permit the stranger to appear only in the most literal sense; that is, to be seen, and not to enable narratives, aesthetics, training, or traditions to be properly or even adequately known by audiences beyond individual cultural communities. When Whittaker expressed admiration, for example, for Toman's directorial skill, he identified him as "one of the most gifted young directors connected with the Multi-Cultural Theatre Association."[58] The comment pays Toman a respect but also patronizes a professional director who had trained at the Academy of the Performing Arts conservatory school in Prague, the Czech's most prestigious theatre school during the 1950s, among a cohort of students who would become stars of Czech theatre and film, to say nothing of the credit Toman deserved for productions he had already directed in Canada. When some years earlier Whittaker had reviewed Nové divadlo's production of *The Importance of Being Earnest*, performed at the Colonnade Theatre on Bloor Street, he called it their first production, and indeed it was their first production – in English. It is telling, as well, that when groups such as Nové divadlo took on canonical Western plays, critics felt the greatest license to pass judgment. Of their *Earnest*, Whittaker wrote, "their taste is impeccable even if their performance is not"[59] (although, inferring from the show's second run a month after its first had closed at the Colonnade, audiences seemed to have found something worthwhile in the production). Toman, who would find it tough to win approval for his scrappy musical cabarets at the Limelight, had as difficult a time with the classics, given comments such as "they simply weren't up to Strindberg"[60] (in an "energetic but superficial *Miss Julie*"); or "the actors will have to relax if they hope to perform Moliere with the breeziness he requires (in an 'out-of-balance Moliere')."[61] In the cultural encounter represented in this reception, the critic became "host," extending a reluctant hospitality to the strangers, welcoming them by virtue of including them in the conversation, while at the same time policing standards to which they could only aspire.

Whittaker couldn't help being positioned at Slavoj Žižek's "empty point of universality" (as mentioned in chapter 1) from which his reviewing would underwrite his own cultural authority. "Whittaker's writing," observe Ric Knowles and Jen Harvie, "employs a developmental teleology in which cultural maturity is always elsewhere, always deferred, and therefore always in need of the paternal care of just such an objective but encouraging supporter as Herbert Whittaker."[62] But the fault really lay with MTAFs themselves. Their politically motivated structure pitted groups against one another in a competition (awards would be doled out for best acting, directing, and so on) that diverted attention from the way they underwrote the authority of the dominant culture. They co-opted minoritized cultures into what Abu-Laban and Gabriel call a "song-and-dance" folkloric multiculturalism that did little to help them be understood and even less to break down barriers between new immigrant artists and the professional arts. And the groups themselves sometimes played along by appealing to a nostalgia that would further align them with a folkloric multiculturalism. Nové divadlo's first production, performed in the lobby at Masaryktown in March, 1970, was Alois Jirásek's *Lucerna*, a classic work of the Czech folk national revival of the nineteenth century that depicts a peasant uprising against foreign landlords. Fast forward to 2012 when the company produced an original folk musical, *Povídky malostranské (Malá Strana Stories)*, based on the nineteenth-century short story cycle about Prague's picturesque Malá Strana quarter. The show's director, Jana Fabiánová, one of the few founding members of Nové divadlo still involved today, wrote in the program for *Povídky malostranské* that she was drawn to the show because it brought her "a very pleasant nostalgia" of her own childhood spent in in Malá Strana. Fabiánová's nostalgia must have been shared in the community because the show saw a larger audience than the company had seen in years.[63] These – and many other possible examples – adopt a retrospective view of simpler times and appeal to the resilient character of the Czech people.

Any "compensatory nostalgia" and any deficiencies in the structure of the multicultural arts both overlooked, however, a whole other dimension to Nové divadlo. Though the group was pleased to appear in the MTAFs, neither their substantial archival material nor the self-histories of the group written by Josef Čermák and František Safertal make much mention of the multicultural festivals or the company's relationship to the wider Canadian theatre audience or industry. In fact, the group never received any funding through the MTAs, still priding itself today in having been financially independent for its entire history. The story Nové divadlo tells about itself is the history of its church basement globalism, of an outward-looking engagement with the global, on and offstage.

CHURCH BASEMENT GLOBALISM

In ways that have gone unnoticed beyond its community, Nové divadlo has been in constant exchange with the Czech and Slovak professional theatre repertoire and industry. The company has regularly invited star professional actors from home to perform alongside its own amateur performers, it has staged important plays of their national traditions, and it has staged North American or Canadian premieres of plays by playwrights banned in their home countries. These visiting actors were not just occasional guests from abroad, but the result of a regular practice of high-profile exchanges. If Nové divadlo's appearances at the MTAFs provide an example of, in Ahmed's formulation, multiculturalism's tendency to "write nation over the bodies of strangers," then the group's globalism demonstrates that the writing is neither exclusive nor indelible. The stranger's position at the threshold can mean – as it did in the critiques of multicultural policy in the 1990s – that they are kept *at* the threshold. But being at the threshold makes it possible to identify a global axis, along which Nové divadlo's activity can be seen as a diasporic extension of the

Czechoslovak theatre ecology rather than as coming from a ghettoized corner of Canada's.

The extent of Nové divadlo's global activities makes evident the exclusions generated by its folkloric framing in Canada. Take, for instance, the appearance on their stages in the 1970s of Jiří Voskovec, a legend of Czech theatre who came of age in the 1930s in the Czech as one half of Voskovec & Werich (V+W), the comic duo comprising the Osvobozené divadlo (Liberated Theatre). V+W became the theatre component of the important Czech avant-garde collective Devětsil, popular with audiences up until the German occupation of the Second World War, which forced V+W and other artists of the avant-garde into silence or exile. Choosing exile, Jiří – or "George" – Voskovec went on to become known to international audiences in Hollywood films, most famously portraying, ironically, the patriotic German-American juror #11 in the classic *Twelve Angry Men.*[64] In 1972 Nové divadlo invited Voskovec to perform alongside its own actors in its production of *Čtyřicet zlosynů a jedno neviňátko (Forty Scoundrels and One Innocent)* and the idea was a hit with the audience of Czech and Slovak immigrants: "For the first time the theatre was completely sold out."[65]

Another impressive achievement was its commissioning and premiering of an original new play by international literary icon Josef Škvorecký. Škvorecký was a Prague Spring émigré who became a professor at the University of Toronto and who, along with his wife, Zdena Salivarová, in 1971 founded the Czech-language Sixty-Eight Publishers, which was an important conduit of *samizdat* culture during the Soviet period.[66] Well known in the Czech for his novels *The Cowards*, *The Engineer of Human Souls* (which won Canada's Governor General's Award in 1984), and *The Swell Season,* Škvorecký became involved with Nové divadlo (his wife was a founding member of the group and appeared in its first production, *Lucerna*, at Masaryktown). In 1980 Škvorecký, by then famous in his homeland and a leading figure of the Czech diaspora, wrote *Bůh do domu (God in Your House)* for Nové divadlo, and the play was staged at the Hart House Theatre in May 1980, directed by Dušan Tóth and Milo Kubik (the play's title is the second half of the Czech aphorism "A guest in your house is a God in your house").[67] Škvorecký, more at home in the novel, leaned on the expertise of the company to develop his play over several versions. The program for the Hart House premiere

2.1 Poster for Nové divadlo's North American premiere of Václav Havel's *Pokoušení* (*Temptation*), staged at Toronto's St Lawrence Centre in October 1988.

announced: "You will hear not only pithy Czech, but delicious Slovak, bad English, proper Canadian, and even unsophisticated Viennese." The company chose Hart House rather than its usual venue because "weight is placed on every word [and] the Hart House theatre allows absolute concentration. Our home is of course still Toman's Limelight" – in other words, this one is special, and we didn't want to distract you by serving you dinner![68]

Perhaps most significant among Nové divadlo's accomplishments have been its productions of plays by the Czech's most famous theatrical export, Václav Havel. In the 1970s and '80s Havel was beginning to be known in Europe for his absurd take on the falsifications of life under authoritarian rule. When in 1979 Nové divadlo staged Havel's *Žebrácká opera (The Beggar's Opera)*, the playwright was serving the longest of his many stays in prison.[69] It would be another decade before Havel became a familiar figure in the West as a champion of democracy and freedom, at which point his plays saw a wave of productions in the UK, the United States, and Canada. Nové divadlo's production of the North American premiere of Havel's *Pokoušení* (*Temptation*), directed by Toman and staged at the St Lawrence Centre in October 1988 on the seventieth anniversary of the founding of the free Czechoslovakia, was a major feat. The play, which reimagines Mephistopheles of the Faust legend in a political allegory about a science institution's seduction of its employees toward "black magic," had been produced one other time in English by the Royal Shakespeare Company and would receive a famous production at the Public Theatre in New York a year after the Nové divadlo production. Given that Nové divadlo had the North American premiere, it was justifiably a point of pride for Josef Čermák: "the original Czech version of the outstanding *Temptation* had its premiere in Toronto, not in Prague ... For Canadian Czechs and Slovaks, it is a privilege to hear our great, indomitable Havel's plays first in the world in our mother tongue."[70] In fact, a nonprofessional production of the play had taken place in the Czech – no doubt under cover of darkness – which Nové divadlo discovered when, to its delight, Havel sent the company a warm response to its invitation to the Toronto production:

> Thank you for your letter. When I learned that you wanted to stage my play, of course I was very pleased. I'll keep my fingers

> crossed that it turns out at least as good as in the English Royal Shakespeare Company (and not so bad as in Vienna). Your invitation was kind, but unfortunately I cannot accept: they would probably let me, but certainly would not let me come back. And let's not risk that. I can only, therefore, keep my fingers crossed. Maybe you would like – just for reference – to see a local amateur video production of "Temptation." It is interesting and some things you could possibly hint about the atmosphere, from which the play originated. A few copies are out there, Dr Janouch or Dr Prečan have them, and possibly Pavel Tigris. If you're wondering, ask for a copy. Yours sincerely, Václav Havel.[71]

Nové divadlo's production of *Temptation* received no notice outside Toronto's Czech community. One wonders whether the case might have been different if it had been staged a year later when, after the Velvet Revolution of 1989, Havel became president of a then still combined Czechoslovakia and an emblem of *glasnost* and democracy. On a visit to Canada and the United States that winter, Havel would meet with US president George H.W. Bush and playwright Arthur Miller – who "welcomed him as the world's first avant-garde president"[72] – and also travel to Toronto, where he would receive an honorary doctorate at York University, address a University of Toronto crowd at Convocation Hall, and meet members of the Czech-Canadian community, including Škvorecký himself.

The seismic shift at home would change the way Czech-Canadians were positioned as strangers in Canada. Havel's mission that winter was to coax the Czech diaspora back to help rebuild the country – a hard sell for a generation soured by a traumatic and sudden exile. Unfortunately for Nové divadlo, Adolf Toman answered Havel's call. In 1991 he sold the Limelight Dinner Theatre and gave up Nové divadlo to work in his hometown of Nymburk, where, in the third act of his life, he restored another foundering theatre to vibrancy.[73] The loss of Toman, coupled with the effects of Velvet Revolution itself, left Nové divadlo to reconsider its purpose. Attendance had fallen, and the group's core members had to figure out how to fill the void that Toman had left. Ironically, the company had been defined by its exile; part of its appeal to its enthusiastic supporters was its ability to maintain a connection to a home from which they were alienated. If Czech Canadians could travel to Prague or Brno and take in the latest production, what was the appeal of participating in productions in Toronto? And for the more committed members of the group, why moonlight in Canadian nonprofessional theatre when there were once again professional opportunities at home? Circumstance had made more visible a division that had probably always been there between two constituencies of strangers: those hoping to return home one day, and those who had settled with no intention of leaving Canada.

At the moment that it might have lost steam, however, the group only became a more active conduit for Czech theatre artists than it had been in the past, first under the leadership of Pavel Král and Tomáš Mašek, and later under Král alone.[74] Král maintained the group's globalism by inviting Czech artists to perform alongside Nové divadlo's nonprofessional volunteers.[75] For instance, after seeing Czech actor Václav Postránecký perform in the Czech National Theatre's production of Nikolai Gogol's *Ženitba (Marriage)*, Král invited Postránecký to perform the same role in a Nové divadlo production, giving the lauded actor the unusual experience of shifting from a state-sponsored national theatre production with professionals in Prague to a nonprofessional production in Toronto. Back in the Czech, Postránecký wrote of his experience in Toronto that "the performances don't have to be good, but if they are, much the better; *Ženitba* at Nové divadlo was excellent."[76] The list of other Czech film and theatre stars appearing in Toronto on Nové divadlo's stage over the last twenty years is impressive.[77] When guest appearances weren't possible, the company would sometimes style local productions after popular ones back home.[78] This proclivity toward imitating productions abroad may reinforce the perception of the company's work as derivative and unworthy of critical notice, but there is something to be said for the international sharing of skills taking place through these exchanges. Moreover, Nové divadlo would augment these productions with original contributions, or would write new versions altogether.[79] And its productions of canonical pieces alongside such international ones would similarly include original elements.[80]

Taken together – guest appearances of major figures of twentieth-century theatre and an accomplished film actor, the premiere of an original play by a luminary of Czech literature, premieres of Havel's plays during the time of his coming to visibility as a political icon, the appearances of dozens of theatre artists reprising roles from professional productions from Czech and Slovak repertory theatres, and a history of original adaptations – Nové divadlo's accomplishments boast an impressive history of practice. I do not acknowledge the group's church basement globalism here to grant it a status it has lacked in Canada – something without which it has carried along just fine – but to illustrate that multiculturalism, a policy intending to recognize strangers, did so in a fashion that occluded their most noteworthy achievements. Such oversights have implications for the way theatre is represented in historical narratives. It is no exaggeration to say that during the Communist period, Nové divadlo was one channel among others through which Czech art could continue to thrive in a time of stagnation and active oppression. The literary culture of the whole Central and Eastern European region was continually reaffirmed in the nineteenth and twentieth centuries by way of its expanding diasporas. Thus, when Přemysl Rut wrote in 1990 that banned Czech theatre "survived at first in private homes, but having been driven even from these it had to put up with a shadow existence, on paper, in *samizdat* plays and magazines,"[81] he was saying that Czech traditions were critically sustained in the underground practices of the Czech diaspora. The same is true within other cultural diasporas, and the breadth and strength of nonprofessional culturally focused theatre in Toronto indicate that the city has played an important role in the dissemination and continued vibrancy of performance traditions globally. This is one illustration of how culture can slip past the national frameworks that have long proscribed it; as Kwame Appiah writes, "much of the culture we want to preserve lives now far away from the cultures that created it."[82] If theatre in Canada has been enriched by the presence of Czechs, theatre in the Czech is also indebted to its passionate advocates in Canada.

CONCLUSION: NOSTALGIA IN A "LIQUID" WORLD

That multiculturalism made it difficult to appreciate the globalism of the nonprofessional culturally focused theatres calls up the need for a meaningful ethics of difference that is not designed merely to legitimize a dominant culture. But despite its adoption into the Canadian national narrative, multiculturalism does not fully determine the activities of strangers who position themselves strategically both inside and outside of it. That is, the performative force of "making strange" can be realized within one cultural sphere but not another, and strangers can manage to occupy both. The influential American sociologist Jeffrey C. Alexander takes exception to the notion that "structural positions" produced by official policies such as multiculturalism guarantee or fix strangeness, and notes the need for an alternative that is conscious of the "active employment of distinctive standards of interpretation" that "make strange."[83] Whittaker, lacking much knowledge of the content or context of what he was evaluating, applied a standard of interpretation that inevitably made strange, and helped realize the ideological agenda of the MTAFs to "write the nation over the body of strangers." But the bodies and lived practices of performance can – and do – bear multiple inscriptions.

For their part, Canada's nonprofessional culturally focused theatre groups could be ambivalent about the way the MTAFs made them strange by positioning them at the threshold of Canadian culture. It must have meant something to members of the groups to perform on large stages in performances attended by mainstream theatre critics. The attraction to participating in these groups was in part the desire to sustain a sense of pride of identity, and, certainly in the case of the Czechs and Slovaks, the wish for affirmation in the wake of a cultural degradation in their homeland. As Jeniva Berger writes, "The number of displaced persons who had survived the trauma of prison camps with the help of amateur dramatics and folklore which strengthened their 'nationhood' in the face of destruction, were legion."[84] A benefit of decoupling the nonprofessional culturally focused theatre from the multicultural agenda is that to do so opens the door to different thinking about what that theatre contributes to the social and cultural life of "world cities" today. Nové divadlo, for instance, provided a means of cultural and linguistic education, which the group has always held as a point of great pride. There is, too, the conviviality of gathering to produce theatre, not so much for its culturally affirmatory dynamics as for the value of community itself, for what Clarke Mackey celebrates as a "conspiracy of the vernacular."[85] It is this, rather than nostalgia or nationalism, that is a source of renewal for these groups in the future. In an interview conducted a decade after he had left Toronto, Toman observed how he had seen the Czech diaspora evolve: "Everything is wider, lots of young people, students come to Toronto. It's more free, it's more open. Not as much nationalism of the Czech now, in modern days it's more social, more on a friendly basis."[86]

Nové divadlo's case illustrates the contradictions of "belonging" in a globalized modernity. As Ash Amin observes, political reactions to the modern condition of mobility and hybridizing identity have been either to "yearn for the security of strong ties" or to "value mobility, exteriority and multiple ties."[87] These seeming opposites do not have to be mutually exclusive. Dismissals of this theatre as nostalgic arise from the older notion of belonging as something immutable and fixed, whereas we might read nostalgia itself differently within Zygmunt Bauman's contemporary "liquid modernity." That is, the nostalgia around which Nové divadlo may coalesce today is less about returning "home" than about a desire for community in a cultural landscape characterized by Bauman's "atomization" of contemporary social life. In other words, it expresses longing for solidity itself. The historian Eric Hobsbawm commented that "never was the word 'community' used more indiscriminately and emptily than in the decades when communities in a sociological sense became hard to find in real life."[88] For Bauman, the problem with nostalgia is its appeal to ontology rather than to ethics; in other words, its understanding that culture exists to make an "is," rather than a "for." As sociologists Chris Till and Tom Campbell write in assessing the value of Bauman's work for the twenty-first century, "Bauman claims that morality is prior to ontology, *for* is before *with*."[89] The new nostalgia may look more like a meta-nostalgia for the idea of cultural fixity and coherence itself, nostalgia for a time when nostalgia *could* satisfy as an antidote for exile. And this may be part of a wider cultural evolution beyond an era that conceived of nostalgia as a sickness, a pathology that arose in a period in which movement was a state of exception.

So, cautiously, we might ask: when might a nostalgia for nostalgia also mean a longing for the stranger to be kept at the threshold, a desire for the stranger to be seen but not known, present at the threshold but as yet unwelcome into the community? And if nation is no longer the arbiter of identity it once was, within which axes of identification do discursive practices of "making strange" still operate? The philosopher Michael Janover draws a distinction between nostalgia and "nostalgias." "Nostalgia," he writes, "is the often conservative and frequently kitsch reverence and re-construction of past forms of life and world." "Nostalgias," on the other hand, can "launch ironic retrievals of the past which can serve as critical measures of the present but in conscious awareness that there can be no return for there is no purely innocent past to return to."[90] Janover's kind of productive self-conscious nostalgia may find its place in the activity of the non-professional culturally focused theatre today, and may allow a fresh look at which cultural values it seeks to preserve or challenge, and which are its aesthetic, social and pedagogical satisfactions.

3

Domesticating the Stranger

To take the stranger as simply present is to overlook and forget the very relationships of social antagonism that produce the stranger as a figure in the first place. Such a fetishization of the stranger, indeed, such an ontology of the stranger as given in and to the world, conceals how "the stranger" comes into being through the marking out of inhabitable spaces, bodies and terrains of knowledge. To talk of the migrant as the stranger is not sufficient.

Sara Ahmed, *Strange Encounters*[1]

In *Strange Encounters*, Sara Ahmed considers how strangers are variously included and excluded in politics, art, and academic research. From many angles, Ahmed considers a fundamental problem that is also at issue here: how we come to "know" others. If a single argument can be said to accumulate in the course of her complex meditation, it is for an urgent need to become more conscious of how strangeness is actively produced. The stranger is not some-body "given in and to the world" (her "some-body" highlighting how bodies become marked as strange) but is generated within and through the strange encounters of her title. An interesting implication of Ahmed's argument is the fact that acts of *including* strangers may be as undesirable as acts of *exclusion*: "incorporation and expulsion can both work simultaneously," she writes, "to fetishize the stranger as the origin of difference."[2] Establishing and maintaining inclusion and exclusion, managing what is or isn't strange, become methods of social control and differentiation. Ahmed seems most keen to learn about "our" desire to know at all, and asks as well which "our" or "we" is bodied forth by the "knowing." Her argument ultimately takes her into the realm of ethics, where she considers not only how strangers are produced through encounter but how the encounter itself *already* assumes the possibility and virtue of "knowing" strangers.

Ahmed's theorizing helps understand how staging strangers developed in Canadian theatre after the overt multiculturalism of the 1970s and '80s had waned. At that time, artists who felt excluded from the predominantly white, Anglo theatre began to form new, professional or semi-professional culturally focused theatre groups that, by working in English and performing in more established theatre spaces, would speak both into cultural communities and beyond them to a broader public. A 1988 issue of *Canadian Theatre Review* on the theme of "Theatre and Ethnicity" took inventory of this new movement, with its editor Natalie Rewa signalling that it represented a departure from "song and dance" multiculturalism: "the question of ethnicity cannot be simply one of heritage preservation and presentation."[3] In another essay in the issue, Cahoots Theatre Projects founder Beverly Yhap says that the new professional groups are "determined to bridge the gap between Multiculturalism that sees arts activities in 'heritage' terms (folk performances) and the professional arts community."[4] In effect, multiculturalism's effort to keep the stranger at the threshold motivated a generation of theatre artists to create a new space of cultural contestation wherein difference could be exposed and interrogated, partly in the form of new plays written in English from minoritized perspectives. Ahmed's argument speaks particularly to a popular narrative that appeared throughout these new plays, the "generational family drama," a story of an immigrant second generation's relationship with its first-generation immigrant parents. Through close readings of three of these plays written over two decades, I consider how they configure Georg Simmel's "here today, stay tomorrow" strangers,[5] who, in this case, are first- and especially second-generation subjects. I want to suggest that the drive toward inclusion manifest in these plays is implicated in the dominant culture's desire to parse the familiar and the strange. As it is for Ahmed, this is ultimately about the kind of knowing that this theatre configures.

Generational family dramas have played a critical role in chronicling the social, cultural, and psychological impact of immigration or exile on immigrant families. They have constituted one means by which "visible minority" artists pushed against the dominant culture and helped create a more pluralized Canadian public. They have also helped to gender that public by foregrounding women as agents of change, women who stand up both to old-world patriarchal cultural practices and to barriers to professional advancement in Canada. To date, these plays have not been appreciated for their analysis of the social implications of globalization on second-generation women. But as much as inclusion is preferable to exclusion, both may essentialize the strangeness of strangers, situating them as the origin of difference and subsuming them into narratives of multiculturalism and the nation to which they might have reason to not fully subscribe. Combining Ahmed's concern with Zygmunt Bauman's cautions against spurious notions of the "public" and "community" evacuated of tension and conflict, there is a possibility that appearances of the stranger may *include* or provide for *recognition* in such a way that is ethically inert. In his book *Land of Strangers*, the geographer Ash Amin, like Ahmed, points to the conditions that produce strangeness in the first place: the mechanisms of ejection and domestication that follow from a "slew of personal and collective labeling conventions – inherited, learnt, absorbed, and practiced – that flow into the moment of encounter … regulated by cognitive and sensory judgments stimulated by the specifics of the occasion."[6] He argues that an urgent need for community in a contemporary context of social alienation in the West has created two equally undesirable possibilities for strangers: that they be either ejected from a community or else marked for domestication.[7] To say that theatre might contribute to the *domestication* of strangers seems hyperbolic, but indeed the domestic is at stake in the generational family drama in multiple senses. The plays are set within the home and among members of families, continuing the well-established tradition of domestic social dramas in the Western theatre; they deal with a domestic, private space set apart from a "public" and a "nation," a space that has historically been gendered as "feminine"; and even the uncomfortably suggestive connotation of the verb form *to domesticate* in the sense of "to make safe" is at issue in the way these dramas may avoid certain uncomfortable realities.

The contradiction of a play that stages a private space on a public stage opens up into a wider contradiction about how the stranger may be simultaneously included and excluded through performance.

On one hand, plays set in the home among families have historically been an important means by which minoritized cultures have had their silenced voices heard on the literal and figurative public stage. "The process of estrangement is the condition for the emergence of a contested community," writes Ahmed, "a community which 'makes a place' in the act of reaching out to the 'out-of-place-ness' of other migrant bodies."[8] So we must adopt Amin's meaning of "domestication" carefully here to point to the stranger's potential "domestication" within multiculturalism, and to a "making safe," in an ethical sense, of avoiding the difficult material realities bearing down on strangers. Balancing these perspectives, it becomes possible that a play can be culturally affirming and empowering while it also supports what sociologist Peter S. Li has called "primordial culture," an "ancient past and museum culture from which minority artifacts can be selectively revived to suit the social needs and the political requirements of the time, under the legitimacy of the dominant culture."[9] In the terms laid out in my first chapter, the generational family drama thus reveals itself to be a site of struggle between a politics of recognition and an ethics of difference. This struggle plays out in the way the way these dramas are self-consciously crafted to address multiple constituencies in the audience. The theatre groups discussed in the previous chapter work in their own language and speak mainly to their own cultural communities; the generational family drama, however, anticipates a mixed audience from within and beyond cultural communities. These plays necessarily perform out to a dominant culture in a new sense, generating the dilemma of placing that dominant culture in a position to somehow be knowing the stranger, where knowing may mean validation, recognition, learning, or welcoming. In what follows, I offer a fresh reading of the generational family drama to re-imagine its satisfactions and challenges within Bauman's liquid modernity.

THE THREAT OF DISCONTINUITY

Betty Quan's play *Mother Tongue* demonstrates a tension between the domestic as a preservationist, psychic refuge from the cultural discontinuities of modernity and a space for an ethical encounter with difference. The play, which premiered at the Firehall Arts Centre in

Vancouver in 1995 and had another production at Factory Theatre in Toronto in 2001, tells the story of a Chinese mother (unnamed in the play), who fled to Canada after facing persecution in China and the death of her husband, and of her daughter Mimi and son Steve, who have grown up in Canada. The immediate conflict in the play is that Mimi must tell her mother that she is going to go to Queen's University in Ontario for graduate school, which will mean that her mother and Steve will have to take care of themselves in her absence. As is characteristic of plays in this tradition, the narrative of *Mother Tongue* is derived from the playwright's own family history: Quan herself is the daughter of Chinese immigrant parents who was encouraged to speak English when she was young.

Quan's drama has been interpreted as an example of the colonized subject's reckoning with the material forces of a colonialist culture.[10] But upon looking at it through the lens of Zygmunt Bauman's "liquid modernity," it also exhibits a palpable anxiety about discontinuity – of culture, history, language, and family. Sociologists have theorized the growing threat of such discontinuities in modern social life, a thesis especially identified with influential sociologist Anthony Giddens, who, in the 1990s, wrote of a widespread, global "detraditionalization."[11] For Giddens and those who have responded to him,[12] discussions of detraditionalization have considered which social values compensate for a loss of continuity with the past. Chief among them for Bauman are the compensatory notions of identity and community, which he sees as less and less capable of maintaining their "solidity." "Gone are the most of the steady and solidly dug-in orientation points," he writes, "which suggested a social setting that was more durable, more secure and more reliable than the timespan of an individual life."[13] For Giddens and Bauman, the family is as another point of psychic orientation in a context of detraditionalization. Giddens's *Runaway World*, a book based on his 1999 BBC lecture series responding to the perception that the modern world is somehow "out of control," devotes a whole chapter to the reactionary American discourse of "family values."[14] Whatever the contemporary source of Giddens's argument, however, his idea builds on a well-established pattern in modernity of investing "family" and the "domestic" sphere with restorative social values.[15]

Generational family dramas display a clear anxiety about cultural discontinuity among first- and second-generation immigrants. While the "song-and-dance" multiculturalism of the previous chapter performed a psychic and cultural "re-traditionalization," the generational family drama translates that anxiety into human and intersubjective terms. In *Mother Tongue* the death of Mimi's father, the children's loss of knowledge about their ancestry and language, and most of all, the forgetting of the family's story of flight and passage, all threaten to dissolve family bonds and a continuity with the past. When, in the play, the mother observes a ritual in honour of the Chinese Qingming Festival, Mimi's indifference provokes her to anger. Speaking at an "ancestral shrine," Mimi's mother compels her to: "obey and serve one's parents when they are alive. Bury them with honour when they are dead. Respect them always. If family does not pay tribute to the dead, they will bring evil upon those still living."[16] Steve, who is deaf and communicates in the play mainly through American Sign Language, watches on, bearing witness along with the audience to the ritualistic act of remembrance, his limited ability to communicate with his mother standing in for his larger disconnection from the past. After the mother reacts badly to Mimi's plan to go to graduate school, she insists: "Go, pay tribute to your paternal grandfather and grandmother. Bi sin. You should've done that when you first came in."[17]

The story of the play seems to say that abandoning this tradition will set the characters adrift in Bauman's "liquid modernity," exiles in a fractured family coping with the loss of an unrecoverable past. References to remembering are constant in the play: "I remember your voice, mother,"[18] "You have made me remember,"[19] "Time to remember all our dead family,"[20] or "Good, you remember the tradition,"[21] as some examples among others. Remembering becomes the family's means of escaping the polyglot confusion of the play's present and retrieving some unity from the past. It is the unfixing of cultural identity itself that constitutes the threat. It is not just that Mimi's choices will break with the past, but that, even within the sanctuary of the family, Mimi, Steve, and their mother will become strangers to one another in the present. Only the ancestral ritual can reconnect the past and present, an effect doubled in the live performance in the sense that the performance of the play itself is a ritual of public remembrance.

Compare *Mother Tongue* with another generational family drama written a decade later, Catherine Hernandez's *Singkil*, produced by Cahoots Theatre and staged at the Factory Theatre in Toronto in 2003. *Singkil* also focuses on the experience of a second-generation daughter – also named Mimi, as if in homage – trying to reconcile her life in Canada with her ancestral past, in this case with her parents' life in the Philippines. But Hernandez's Mimi picks up where Quan's left off insofar this Mimi, and her father, are acclimatized to life in Canada – Mimi after having grown up there entirely and Nestor after having immigrated in the 1970s. Hernandez's Mimi, like Quan's, struggles to come to terms with an absent parent and her severed connection with ancestry and tradition. The play begins with Mimi's mother, Maria, having just passed away. When her mother's friend Norma comes to visit from the Philippines, Mimi's unhappy relationship with her late mother is forced out into the open. The play alternates between scenes set in the present between Mimi, Norma, Nestor, and Mimi's boyfriend, Chase, and those set in the past during her parents' courtship, their immigration to Toronto, and with friends Norma and Maria.

Also as in *Mother Tongue*, the past is aligned with a tradition that Mimi must recover not only in order to come to terms with her mother's death but, by extension, also to come to terms with the culture and ancestry that her mother represents. Completing the connection between the domestic and the traditional is the mother's strong identification in the play as a dancer of the Singkil, a traditional Philippine dance based on the legend of a Muslim princess who escapes death in an earthquake by dancing herself to safety. Having little interest in her mother or her past, Mimi had rejected the dance while her mother was alive, but when a Sari manok – the ornate headdress worn by a Singkil dancer – surfaces among her mother's belongings in the play, it asserts a material presence that Mimi is unable to suppress. The symbolism is heavily played in a dream sequence in which Mimi is handed the Sari manok by a cab driver, who accidentally drops it, smashing it on the floor; Mimi awakens screaming at her boyfriend, Chase, "Why did you break it!?"[22] In *Singkil*'s own culminating moment, when Mimi finally puts to words her feeling that her mother hated her because her mother was in a loveless marriage with her father, Nestor, the past quite literally moves in to alleviate Mimi's anxiety when Norma shows her an old photo of her mother. The photo, taken of her mother after she had immigrated to Toronto in 1974, features her dancing the Singkil at the Philippine Consulate in Toronto. The photo, it turns out, was taken when her mother was two months' pregnant with Mimi. The fact of her mother's momentary happiness and pride while bearing the biological connection to her daughter unravels Mimi's resentment and inclines her toward forgiveness.

The play thus places responsibility on the second-generation subject for the recovery of Li's "primordial culture," an ontologically fixed and authentic culture located in an ancestral past. This would seem to be a widespread trope in the literature of the Asian American diaspora; Daphne Lei has observed of Asian American theatre that, "the unobtainable homeland and unquenchable nostalgia of the Issei (the first generation) has been a constant dramatic device in the genre."[23] As discussed at the end of the previous chapter, however, performance can make of nostalgia something more than a regressive or compensatory force. However much *Mother Tongue* or *Singkil* may "primordialize" the family's culture, these plays also depart from "song-and-dance" multiculturalism by directly addressing the stranger's experience of living at the threshold. The plays neither strictly "eject" nor "domesticate" the stranger but take on the perspective of the stranger trying to live meaningfully at the threshold within multiple worlds and competing obligations. Although the family's culture is something fixed in the past, the plays propose that this past be kept alive in the present through ritualistic acts of remembrance. As Ahmed reminds us, airing the perspective of migrants in this fashion "does not take place through the heroic act of an individual, but in the forming of communities that create multiple identifications through collective acts of *remembering* in the absence of a shared knowledge or familiar terrain."[24]

Gender is also a critical vector of how strangers are made to appear in these dramas. As a story of an immigrant daughter leaving home to pursue a career, *Mother Tongue* offers a strong female figure staking a claim on space outside the domestic sphere. "Open the curtains!" Mimi demands of her mother in a revolt against the obligations of family. This scenario of the immigrant female subject balancing commitments to home and career, was, as Shelley Scott has observed, "a frequent theme in 1970s and '80s British, American and Canadian feminist writing."[25] In their analysis of women's intercultural performance, Julie Holledge and Joanne Tomkins note that postcolonial women writers create an "imaginary space between 'home' and 'homelessness'" with the potential to be "significantly empowering."[26] The generational family drama has typically had strong female protagonists that create the kind of emancipatory imaginary space the authors imagine. Drawing on Elizabeth Grosz's notion of *chora*,[27] Holledge and Tomkins assert that these spaces implicate women in spaces usually occupied by men, or otherwise generate new ways of inhabiting space and bodies.[28] They imagine how "memory spaces" that express a "longing for a lost home, in the sense of a physical dwelling, a national or cultural site, and a psychic location of safety and comfort"[29] allow a symbolic negotiation of evolving, gendered social and familial relations. In the case of the generational family drama, it is understandable that Canadian playwrights would have addressed the experience gap between generations by constituting a sense of home through visions of ancestral and cultural pasts. *Mother Tongue* is an example of Grosz's *chora* in the sense that the play provided a stage for Quan and the immigrant Canadian subject to symbolically claim a place in the cultural landscape, a stage with different possibilities than those available to the nonprofessional culturally focused groups discussed in the previous chapter. The political possibility is a counterpoint to Giddens and Bauman's conservative view of the domestic as a compensatory refuge from globalized modernity. As Bahira Sherif Trask illustrates in her richly researched book *Globalization and Families*, the traditional gendering of the private and public is currently in significant revision, and the different choices available to women in families around the world illustrate the uneven consequences of globalization.[30]

For its part, *Mother Tongue* may also deliver a difficult and indeterminate ethics. Understanding across difference is challenged both within the play and between the stage and audience. The characters of the play all face obstacles to speaking, listening, and truly being heard, as in Steve's monologue in which he describes his struggle to be heard by his non-deaf family members: "Air forming into sounds I can't hear. Into words I can't speak. Into sentences no one will listen to."[31] The play literalizes barriers to intercultural communication by having the mother, Mimi, and Steve speak predominantly in Cantonese, English, and American Sign Language respectively, an example of what Marvin Carlson calls "macaronic theatre," performed in multiple languages.[32] This required Quan to carefully construct the drama so as to be intelligible to audiences members who speak any of these languages alone. It isn't merely for the sake of verisimilitude that Quan has the characters flipping between languages; the choice thematically orients the play around communication and openly flags the multiple audiences to which it addresses itself. The characters are frustrated by their inability to adequately speak to one another and the audience:

> *(STEVE faces the audience as if facing a mirror.)* My name is Steve Chan. *(He is getting angry.)* My name is Steve Chan. I cannot hear you. My sister, sister, sister. *(The deaf have particular difficulty with sibilant words. This frustrates STEVE.)* Sister! Sister! *(STEVE puts his hand over his throat; we move into his inner voice)* I remember …[33]

At this point in the play Steve overcomes the barriers to communication and understanding for those not familiar with ASL by delivering a speech in English. In the play's final moments, language becomes momentarily more intelligible in the family when Steve speaks English and signs his words simultaneously and Mimi repeats her mother's Cantonese words in English. A parable told in the play about a "Jingwei" bird that builds a bridge across the ocean pebble by pebble becomes symbolic of the family's incremental – though incomplete and potentially impossible – process of coming to know one another and their shared history.[34] The parable serves also as a metaphor for ethical encounter with strangers in theatre, expressing a compulsion toward knowing in spite of its indeterminacy and slow progress.

Mother Tongue also plays out indeterminacy at the level of choices in a manner that is characteristic of the generational family drama: both the first generation's lack of choice in the desire to leave home, and the second generation's relative freedom to choose a life for themselves. The different choices of the generations become the crux of the misunderstanding between Mimi and her mother:

MIMI: You came all the way across the Pacific Ocean. All by yourself. That's farther than I have to go.
MOTHER: *(Chinese)* I had no choice!
MIMI: Then let me choose what I want to do![35]

Quan also cleverly leaves a choice hanging in the balance in the play's final moment. In it, the three family members occupy separate spaces onstage "each in his/her individual lights," in which "their inner voices speak to one another but they are physically unaware of each other."[36] The mother leaves her spotlight to approach Steve, offering him an orange from the ancestral altar, a symbol of the tradition and family memory under threat of rupture in the play. But the moment delivers no compensatory reconciliation. The final stage directions maintain Steve's, and the family's, unresolved conflict: *"Her hands holds out the orange.* STEVE *is hesitant to take it.* MOTHER *reaches out again, this time using her other hand to force* STEVE *to face her. Lights Out. The End."*[37]

INDIVIDUAL ADJUSTMENT TO INEVITABLE REALITIES

Ahmed argues for encounters with the stranger that are "always and already a movement away from home as such," so that they resist any "stasis of being."[38] In just this way, that final image in *Mother Tongue* denies the movement toward home, refuses to deliver the past to the present as a satisfying remedy to the family crisis. The refusal becomes ethical for being indeterminate – although one could ask whether a choice between the past and present, tradition and modernity, reductively suggests that these are mutually exclusive options. Even if so, the play has presented cultural difference as something *at issue*, the stranger as a figure contemplating itself in its unsettled and unsettling position at the threshold.

Singkil, by contrast, is resolute about the stranger's movement toward "home." Where *Mother Tongue*'s ending leaves open whether or not Steve will accept his Mother's offer, and by implication take an interest in the family's past and tradition, *Singkil*'s ending is realized in a series of closing scenes in which Mimi makes peace with her mother, then her father, then Norma, and then her boyfriend, Chase. In the first of these scenes, Mimi confronts her mother at her grave:

"Did you hear that, Mom? I'm going to forgive you now. I'm going to take everything that stings, that throbs and hurts inside my heart, and let it go. I'm going to forgive and be happy."[39] She goes on to release the long-simmering tension with her father by recalling a moment when they went camping together and felt out of place as the only "brown" people on the campsite. "Why did we go camping?" Mimi asks, to which her father responds, "To be together," at which point "*the ghost of Maria, who has entered the scene, places her hand on Nestor's.*"[40] In the play's last scene, Mimi's transformative acceptance is complete as she walks in and performs the Singkil dance for her father:

> MIMI *enters in full traditional Singkil costume, wearing her mother's Sari manok and using her mother's fans. The sound of* MIMI*'s ankle bells awaken something inside* NESTOR. *He knows what is being shown to him. She begins the dance. The height of the dance is broken when, unbeknownst to everyone on stage except for* NESTOR, MARIA *enters and sits on a chair beside him. She holds his hand.*[41]

This closing sequence of scenes celebrates continuity, guaranteeing it with a sense of total emotional closure. "Keep on dancing, Norma," says the ghostly Maria.[42]

Singkil's resolution may offer a satisfying cultural affirmation and hope for a way forward for a second generation trying to deal with the enormous challenges faced by the generation before it. As Eleanor Ty writes of the play: "the ending is significant because it suggests an embracing rather than a rejection of the father, the mother, and the motherland. The play demonstrates that, unlike their immigrant parents, second generation children want more out of life."[43] But does the individual self-realization of the play's conclusion satisfy as a resolution to its conflict? In Quan's drama, the challenges of the second generation are social and structural; in Hernandez's drama they are psychological. As a consequence, discontinuity is bound up with Mimi's resentment toward her mother and her decision about whether to forgive her. For the audience, this creates an unambiguous psychological arc in which Mimi's emotional resolution becomes a wider accommodation to any anxieties wrought by the condition of immigration, exile, or discontinuity. As mentioned in the discussion in chapter 1, the potential trouble here is what Ric Knowles refers to as an "individual adjustment to inevitable realities," a variant of a wider sociological critique of the "individualization" or "atomization" of politics. Bauman is similarly concerned with how cultural "becoming" substitutes for politics a "life-politics" that sentimentalizes culture and avoids any meaningful challenge to social injustice or meaningful encounter with difference. In liquid modernity, Bauman writes, "illnesses are individual, and so is the therapy ... Worries are private, and so are the means to fight them off."[44] Do the material or ideological conditions shaping a family's history become, in the process, Knowles's "inevitable realities" that the audience, along with Mimi, are to accept? I raise the question not to undermine the power of Mimi's coming into self-possession as a Filipino Canadian or as a woman, nor to devalue the experience of those in the audience who will identify with Mimi's effort to make peace with her past, but to point out what does not go discussed in the play. No mention is made, for instance, of why the family left the Philippines, or the fact that Nestor's training wasn't recognized in Canada, forcing him to work in manual labour, or the barriers Mimi faces to establishing a career in Canada as a second-generation immigrant. To confront those conditions could move the play toward different territory in ethical terms, potentially implicating its audience in the socio-cultural circumstances that have shaped the family's story. Recalling the idea of an ethics of difference for theatre which is meaningful at the point of being both difficult and indeterminate, what is supposed to be satisfying about *Singkil*'s narrative is also what is disconcerting about it: how satisfyingly resolved its tensions are for its audience, how neatly the restoration of ancestral continuity proposes to suture the wounds of the past and the present. Is the play perhaps cynical in its acceptance that any of the circumstances that produced its dramatic situation can be resolved by an act of individual forgiveness?

Singkil's moral poetics presents difference as something not to be exposed and confronted, but to be accepted and offered up for public recognition. As I wrote in my first chapter, the moral is not without political potential, and here, *Singkil*'s celebration of a woman reconciling with her public and private roles still presents the immigrant family as a site of ideological struggle with globalized modernity.[45] It therefore refutes the strict sociological view that the family can compensate for modern alienation, and draws attention to how immigrant families in particular, anywhere in the world, are caught between the demands of the past and those of the present. On the basis of sociological research of women's lives around the world, Bahira Sherif Trask argues that families are in fact not uniformly disintegrating and disappearing, but becoming – or perhaps are continuing to be – the front line of response to global forces.[46] Yvonne Hodkinson, for her part, has identified a focus on isolation and separation from the public sphere across Canadian drama by women playwrights, plays in which the protagonists' "misery in the domestic home becomes a metaphor for female isolation."[47] Similarly, Scott, writing about Marjorie Chan's plays, has noted how Chan's generations of women, finding themselves "diminished by a patriarchal society," discover ways "to remember and support each other."[48] Thus the critique that *Mother Tongue* and *Singkil* offer a morally affirmative "individual adjustment to inevitable realities" is tempered by the fact of Mimi's discovering in the family a solidarity that is politically empowering – just the kind of collective solidarity Bauman laments. The "opening the curtains" of Quan's Mimi avoids being strictly about cultural self-realization by simultaneously constituting a demand for inclusion in the public sphere and nation.

In these generational family dramas, strangers negotiate between private and public, the individual and the community, the local and the global. As historian Amy Kaplan has written, considering the historical place of the domestic in relation to nation, "private domesticity plays a key role in defining public domesticity."[49] Ahmed here usefully points to the manner in which the stranger is *already* conditioned by the circumstances of his or her encounter. An important dimension of this encounter, beyond the narratives and poetics of the plays, is the diversity of the audience that the plays anticipate: first- and second-generation Canadians within their community, those from other minoritized communities who may strongly identify with their themes, and those who see themselves outside the experience represented in them. The plays thus exhibit something like W.E.B. DuBois's "double-consciousness,"[50] the sense of simultaneously inhabiting one's body on one's own terms while also being hailed by the dominant culture. The way in which they seize visibility "on their own terms" is critical. As discussed in the last chapter, the stranger's pursuit of hospitality in a "public" or "nation" may underwrite the authority of the dominant culture positioned to do the "welcoming." Generational family dramas inevitably serve a politics of recognition by configuring the encounter with strangers as a bid for inclusion. At the same time, they may wish to not be labelled as "ethnic" plays (or, in this case, as "women's plays") but as *plays* that may be considered and valued like any others. "My concern with tracing the relations of knowledge that allow the stranger to enter the community as a figure," writes Ahmed, "has been precisely to situate figurable strangers within the relations of force and authorization bound up with the 'who' that knows."[51] The knowing "who" in this case is multiple, generating overlapping demands for recognition and an ethics of difference. In my reading of the generational family drama, the "who" that knows is both the dominant culture that recognizes or welcomes the stranger into the community of the nation and a "who" that grapples with, and embraces, the contradictions of plural identifications and loyalties in a globalized modernity.

DOMESTICATION AS "MAKING SAFE"

Bauman worries about a public in which "the differences inside, unlike the differences outside, are tamed, sanitized, guaranteed to come free of dangerous ingredients – and so be unthreatening."[52] While a global and intersectional perspective on *Mother Tongue* and *Singkil* blunts the sociological critique of a depoliticized, atomized individuality, *Mother Tongue* and *Singkil* at the same time do not much confront the tensions, challenges, prejudices, and structural limitations that would make life difficult for the stranger as a first- or second-generation immigrant subject. There remains some extent to which both plays present difference without difference; that is, they create a dramatic world domesticated in the sense of having been "made safe." The domestic in this instance is interesting in relation to the stranger because, in the same way that the concept of the stranger necessarily points to a process of making strange, the domestic connotes a familiar and safe space set in opposition to something presumed to be foreign and wild. Like the concept of culture itself, the domestic associates with agriculture, where it signals a power relationship, as in its verb form, which means "to tame from a wild and natural condition into a more manageable one."

Ins Choi's highly successful *Kim's Convenience*, another generational family drama, gives us an opportunity to ask whether its strangers are "domesticated" in this sense. First developed with Toronto's Fu-Gen Asian Canadian Theatre Company between 2005 and 2011 and premiered in 2011 at the Toronto Fringe Festival, *Kim's Convenience* went on to win the Fringe's New Play Contest and the Patron's Pick, was picked up by Toronto's classical repertory company Soulpepper in 2012 and remounted for two additional runs, toured across Canada, appearing in London, Port Hope, Hamilton, Ottawa, Calgary, Winnipeg, and Vancouver, and had an additional run at Soulpepper in late 2014. To top it off, the play was developed into a CBC television series for the CBC that premiered in October 2016.[53] This extraordinary trajectory for a Canadian play, coupled with its near-unanimous critical praise, demonstrates that audiences remain interested in the themes of the generational family drama.

As in the plays discussed earlier, *Kim's Convenience* centres on an immigrant family, here of Korean Canadians, and much of the focus falls on a second-generation daughter. It owes an obvious debt to plays such as *Mother Tongue* and *Singkil*, despite Soulpepper artistic director Albert Schultz's statement in his Preface to the published text of the play that "for many of this generation, the first step of that journey to cultural confidence will be through the door that Ins Choi has opened."[54] Choi has clearly been the beneficiary of other theatre artists' efforts to create a space for minoritized voices on the stage, one of whom, actor/playwright Jean Yoon, performed the mother of the family, Umma, in the first Soulpepper run of the play. The "daughter" of this play, Janet, like Mimi in *Singkil*, has grown up in Canada and is trying to make a career while she struggles with family history and obligations. In *Kim's Convenience* (hereafter, *Kim's*), Janet faces a choice between a career in photography and taking over the family convenience store of the title. Her lack of interest in the store places its fate in the hands of her brother Jung, who is estranged from the family after a having had violent fight with his father that landed him in the hospital fifteen years before the play's action. Two narrative threads build toward a utopian ending: one that sees Janet coupled with a young black police officer named Alex, whom she knew from high school, and another that sees Jung emerge from his self-imposed exile from the family to confront and forgive his abusive father. The double resolution features a daughter in a mixed-race relationship and a son recognizing his father's sacrifice and guaranteeing continuity by deciding to take up the honourable familial duty.

Kim's differs from the earlier plays for being a comedy, a television sitcom-like blend of farce and sentimentality. Absent are the poetic-realist elements of earlier generational family dramas, along with the symbolically charged old-world backdrop they dramatized. Choi's play opts instead for stylistic realism, supported by Ken MacKenzie's hyper-realistic convenience store setting in the Soulpepper production, replete with authentic vintage signs and aisles of snacks. The setting and tone of the drama are reminiscent of 1970s or '80s comedies that played lightly the experience of eccentric, "fish-out-of-water" immigrants. As J. Kelly Nestruck wrote presciently in his *Globe and Mail* review of the first Soulpepper production, "*Kim's Convenience* reminds me of those socially relevant 1970s comedies produced by Norman Lear – or Canada's King of Kensington. Come to think of it, you can imagine this being the pilot for a CBC remake: *Kim's of Regent Park.*"[55] For some critics, the play's disarming comic charm forgave any failure to deal with real cultural politics or the actual situation of Korean Canadians. Joff Schmidt, for example, wrote: "*Kim's Convenience* is not the definitive study of generational conflict in immigrant families in Canada, but that's not what it's trying to be. It's heartfelt and it's laugh-out-loud funny and it's honest. And I'll buy that any day."[56] But what is Schmidt claiming the play is "honest" about? Conspicuously absent in reviews of *Kim's* are any comments on its stereotyped characterizations: Rich is an uneducated black man who speaks in slang and has trouble understanding basic conversation; Mike, a black man "with a thick Jamaican accent," is caught stealing from the store; and Appa's stereotypically clipped Korean accent in English, along with his constant cultural and linguistic gaffes, is a source of humour throughout the play. Appa's portrayal by Paul Lee was widely praised in reviews, evidently comfortable with the fact of Appa being a walking, breathing stereotype of a stern Asian parent, whose racism toward other minoritized cultures expects to be excused by the play's Russell Peters–like humour.

The fact that *Kim's* is a comedy may, to some audience members, be enough to excuse its broad characterizations. It would also be absurd and unfair to expect that any story told from the perspective of a minoritized culture has an obligation to address the roots of prejudice or racism. Still, the conspicuously wide berth *Kim's* takes around any uncomfortable social realities seems to me to indicate an unsettling wider discomfort with the stranger. Consider, for instance, Appa's explanation to Janet of how to recognize a thief in the store, which involves a personal system of classifying customers by race, gender, sexual orientation, and physical features to predict whether they will, as Appa puts it, "steal or no steal."[57] Janet's dismissive laughter at Appa in this sequence and her characterization of her father as "awkwardly racist"[58] seem to expect an audience that will see – or wish to see – Appa as a well-meaning dinosaur with outdated attitudes in comparison to the younger generation's own cultural open-mindedness. When I saw this sequence in performance, I wanted to think that the laughs it generated were self-consciously uncomfortable, signalling a small, tacit acknowledgment in the audience of some latent, real-world racism. My worry, however, was that on the contrary, the laughter confirmed and celebrated a society that had successfully rid itself of racial friction. Speaking for myself, I laughed, but then left the theatre feeling as if I had been asked to adopt a self-congratulatory stance, complicit, perhaps, in what Smaro Kamboureli has discussed as "multiculturalism fatigue," the comfortable view within the dominant culture that multiculturalism "has already fulfilled, if not exceeded, its mandate."[59] If you add up the dismissal of Appa's racism with other elements of the play, for instance Janet's interracial relationship and the black police officer Alex's intimate knowledge of Korean food, *Kim's* presents an image of the diverse, global city, "the most multicultural city in the world," in which, especially for a younger generation, racism is a thing of the past.

There actually is a social justice critique in *Kim's*, but it is a critique that exacerbates the problem of how it positions its audience. The play's action is propelled by the possibility of Appa selling the store to a developer, such that the store becomes a platform for resistance to the massive economic force of urban redevelopment. This could be a particularly resonant critique in Toronto on account of the redevel opment of Regent Park, a notoriously underserved social housing project that underwent a large-scale redevelopment during the period of *Kim's* tours and remounts. This conflict, however, backgrounded and broadly drawn, is a woolly critique of neoliberal globalization. It is an example of Doreen Massey's "victimizing" story, which invests the local with warm, feel-good values in opposition to the cold, corporate vision of globalization.[60] The threat to discontinuity here is amplified by a ruthless capitalism bearing down on the store, on the Kims' church, which has had to relocate to the suburbs, and also on Janet and Jung, who struggle to piece together a career when stable employment appears to be out of reach. This background narrative further underscores the stranger's domestication by anticipating a knowing "who": the sense that the "Kims' story" is "everyone's story." Whereas the discontinuities of *Mother Tongue* and *Singkil* are closely tied to specific cultural histories, myths, and traditions, *Kim's* makes a more direct bid to universalize the drama into a greater narrative about the discontinuity of modernity and a lack of social connection of the sort that the in-person interactions of a local convenience store make possible. Should the convenience store be lost, it would be more than a loss to the Kims or to the Korean Canadian community (which, one might imagine, may have ambivalent feelings about romanticizing the life of a small business owner working long hours) but a loss to society at large. Some "we" seems to own the convenience store, a "we" that stands to lose something if it becomes a Walmart. When in the play Appa is offered a handsome sum for his business by a developer, he replies: "This is very generous Mr. Kim, but no. This community need me. Even if Walmart moving in, people in neighbourhood need this store."[61]

What are the implications for this universalizing gesture for the way *Kim's* implicates its audience? If *Kim's* makes a bid for the stranger's inclusion in the imagined community of the nation, has it come at the cost of the stranger's domestication? The laughs at *Kim's* are earned by Choi and the play's performers, but they require accepting some comforting, or discomfiting, truths. What of the family's history, of Appa's path to being a convenience store owner, of the casual racism he faces – or doles out? Though the play has clearly offered something valuable to a Korean Canadian audience, and something as well to a broader immigrant audience that identifies with the play's light-hearted moments of cultural and generational misunderstanding, *Kim's* is also calculated to speak beyond those audiences. Whatever muted social critique it may contain, it may also have domesticated the stranger in the sense of "making safe" by showing that the Kim family is happy enough with its lot and that the play's audience can continue on as before. Albert Schultz, addressing, one imagines, his imagined audience at Soulpepper, draws out this horizon of expectations in his Preface to the published play text:

> Its subject matter is extremely familiar. What is remarkable about the play is that despite this familiarity, it feels so original. And it feels very Canadian … For anyone who has watched this play, it will be impossible to pick up a litre of milk at the corner store without wondering what story is unfolding behind the cash register. Every time we hear the electronic doorbell announce our departure, we will think about the lives we have left behind.[62]

Schultz's framing of the play as "extremely" familiar – a word here connoting both the "known" and "familial" – indicates that he expects the audience will recognize the dramaturgical formula of the generational family drama. Its "feeling Canadian" suggests that its power is emotional, and that whatever difference the play might offer can be accommodated into the multicultural Canadian subject that Schultz implicitly evokes with his "we." His framing signals to Soulpepper's largely white audience that this won't be an "ethnic" play but something "Canadian" and therefore, presumably, still of interest. To its "ethnic" (partially Korean Canadian) audience, it signals that the play includes them in the Canadian national mosaic, a gesture seemingly presuming Schultz's own cultural authority to grant that legitimacy. Schultz also underscores the play's Canadianness to highlight its exceptionality in his theatre company's otherwise mainly canonical, Euro-American repertoire. The "anyone" of the statement most obviously anticipates a non-immigrant audience, and clearly identifies the extent of the political aspiration of the play: that this "anyone" should give a passing thought to the immigrant experience. Schultz makes his brand of universalism most clear in an additional comment that "the magic depth to which [Choi] has taken this specificity is the same depth from which the play's universality is sprung. This play, on hearing, becomes *our story* about *our family* in *our community*."[63] Well-meaning as it may be, Schultz's gesture of hospitality toward the stranger implies an "our" possessed of the performative power to include the stranger here both in the Euro-American dramatic canon of "classics" and in the multicultural Canadian nation. His idea that we can all be "different" and be "united" as well would not be out of place as a director's note in a program for the multicultural festivals of the 1970s, which were oriented around a similarly totalizing cultural claim.

All of this may say more about Schultz and Soulpepper than Choi's play, but the play does make itself vulnerable to this universalizing gesture by prompting its audience to laugh at the fact that there really was a struggle for recognition in first place, as when Janet brings up the matter of generational choice at issue in all the plays of the tradition:

> JANET: Look, Appa, you did what you had to do, right? And I appreciate that. I do. But didn't you do what you had to do so I wouldn't have to do what I had to do but could choose what I wanted to do?
>
> APPA: What?

Such oblique and playful references to prejudice make the play susceptible to a cultural discourse that diverts attention away from "the roots of mutual distrust and disagreement," to use the words Bauman uses to critique multiculturalism itself.[64] The broad community it portrays domesticates the stranger's difference in a universal gesture that would bring all members of the audience together as victims of a terrific and overwhelming neoliberal globalization – what Nancy Fraser dubs the "neoliberal tsunami" version of globalization.[65] The poetics of the play and its relationship with the audience are a long way from difficult or indeterminate. The play generates a sense of community within the audience it addresses that Bauman would consider antithetical to his ethical public: "In a community, we all understand each other well, we may trust what we hear, we are safe most of the time and hardly ever puzzled or taken aback. We are never strangers to each other."[66]

CONCLUSION: A NEAR SPHERE OF MORAL CONCERN

I have written elsewhere about how the ways of doing and writing ethnography in anthropology relate to the history of intercultural encounter in performance, in particular about how modernist or colonial ways of looking continue to haunt acts of theatrical spectatorship across cultures.[67] Reaching out to anthropology for her critique in *Strange Encounters*, Sara Ahmed discusses how the ethnographic gesture of the act of going to learn about others already presumes the possibility of knowing others. This, she argues, is already a domestication because it imagines that the experience or situation of strangers can be communicated, understood, taken on, known. "The idea of 'themselves' is *created* through such an anthropological demand (what is it like for them?): a creation which *figures* the stranger insofar as the stranger poses a crisis for anthropological knowledge."[68] The plays discussed in this chapter have presented themselves to heterogeneous audiences as crises of identity, as public social dramas in which the possibility of self-realized identity prefigures the stranger as knowable. The presumption of knowability calls up a particular "we" doing the knowing, where knowing has the potential to become a gesture of hospitality absented of a desire to confront any unsavoury aspects of encounter across difference – Fraser's "recognition without distribution."[69]

Kim's Convenience has fun with the tradition of the generational family drama and can claim to have refreshed the tradition for a millennial generation that is anxious, in the way that Jung is, about over-education and under-employment. Yet it is worth asking whether it has had to be a frictionless presentation of difference that invites its audience into a post-racial fantasy wherein racism is a thing of the past. Difference is set aside, "social antagonism" – in Ahmed's phrase – is placed beyond view, a product only of forces to which any audience members would find themselves opposed, such as the force of capitalist greed or relentless urban redevelopment. Whereas *Mother Tongue* and *Singkil* both reclaim the private space of the generational family drama as an important, and gendered, public drama, *Kim's* occupies a more conflicted place in the matrix of recognition and ethics. A different reading of the gesture toward the universal, its sense that "we" are all the Kims' family, is that it speaks of Choi's, and perhaps Soulpepper's and the audience's wish to depart from single-ethnicity politics and position the play within a humanist discourse in which a drama about the Korean Canadian experience can be made to be a drama for "us" in the same way that any drama might. But without reducing this discussion to a simple investment in either particularity or universalism, the question arises as to whether the play has had to accommodate itself to an audience for whom it needed to be non-confrontational and palatable, and whether it therefore validates the dominant culture's gesture of hospitality toward a domesticated stranger.

My critique is thus not directed at Choi's play – which is ably crafted and has been warmly accepted by audiences for good reasons – so much as toward the situation of encounter in which it is implicated. My concern is that there has been a "we" who plays "host" in this encounter, a "we" requiring the stranger to be unthreatening in order to gain "entry" to the "home," a "we" for whom the price of recognition is an erasure. While recognition has its force, it also may allow the portion of its audience that enjoys the privileges of membership in the dominant culture to sidestep the question of its own implication or complicity in systems of exclusion. If one accepts that recognition may function in this way, then it is worth asking how it might be made to function differently. How, in staging strangers, can theatre on the Canadian stage provide for diverse perspectives in the public sphere and their equal representation, while still being also able broach contentious matters of difference, such as systemic barriers to opportunity, persistent racism, or the differential effects of neoliberal capitalism on minoritized communities? In the terms used in chapter 1, how can this theatre hold a politics of recognition and an ethics of difference in balance? It matters, because there remains a critical need for diverse perspectives and more equal cultural representation on Canadian stages. Observing a similar tension between recognition and ethics, feminist theorists of performance have noted the need for solutions. Jill Dolan observes that even while theorists "debate the efficacy of theater as mimesis … giving up the notion of theater as a place to image those who are elsewhere erased is difficult."[70] Shelley Scott is correct in writing that recognition in Canadian theatre remains important no matter its theoretical problems: "Those who have yet to be adequately represented onstage and who have seldom had the opportunity to see themselves as subjects in the theatre will not be willing to give this up as a goal, no matter how theoretically problematic the construction of subjecthood may be."[71]

This theoretical problem – the desire to simultaneously build community and deconstruct identity – is becoming more apparent as the generational family drama takes up more global settings and subjects. Take, for instance, Nina Lee Aquino's 2013 play *Every Letter Counts*, staged in 2013 at Toronto's Factory Theatre. As in the plays discussed above, *Every Letter Counts* features a female protagonist named Bunny who experiences a crisis of identity implicating her family's past, in this case in the Philippines, and the play opens with the question "Who am I?" repeated, in the Factory production, on voice-over, signalling a continuity with the tradition. *Every Letter Counts* was treated harshly by some critics; they found its symbolism overplayed, its documentary and realistic styles clashing, and Bunny's resentment, directed as in the earlier plays toward a parent, unconvincing.[72] In its defence, however, I would argue that the play was criticized for something larger than itself: the difficulty of resizing an established dramaturgical form – the generational family drama – to address global subjects and distant strangers. Critics sensed the problem, but appeared to lack the perspective to name it. Robert Cushman, for instance, wrote, "Either this play is telling the wrong story or it's telling the right one in the wrong way."[73] The problem Cushman wasn't naming lay in the fact of the play's conflicting narratives: one about a character seeking resolution with her family, and another one about a historical political situation in the Philippines that calls up a different relationship of knowing and care with an unfamiliar context. In a similar vein, another generational family drama representing an overt turn toward the global is Theatrefront's play *RETURN: The Sarajevo Project*, developed in a series of workshops in both Toronto and Sarajevo, Bosnia and Herzegovina, between 2003 and 2005. In *RETURN*, Tarik, a Bosnian Canadian, returns to Sarajevo to reconcile with his family whom he had fled a decade earlier at the outbreak of war. The drama of the play arises from Tarik's naïve wish to relocate his family to Canada colliding with the realities of a family who see themselves as inextricably Bosnian, and who have held onto resentments about Tarik's abandonment. As far as this goes, the play carries on the tradition of plays in which global dislocation produces a domestic and ontological rupture in identity that must be restored. But *RETURN* packs into the generational family drama extra freight in the form of heavy and unresolved moral questions about Western complacency and interventionism in global conflict.

These plays demonstrate the persistence of dramaturgical form in Canada in the face of shifting sociological conditions. The generational family drama came into being to express the second-generation immigrant's experience, but it is having to refit itself to a new cultural moment marked by an interest in knowing both proximate and distant strangers. Bauman, in characteristic fashion, is pessimistic about the possibility that existing public spaces and forms can "scale-up" to fit the new global landscape: "Those public stages, constructed originally for the nation-and-state political purposes, remain stubbornly local – whereas contemporary drama is humanity-wide, and so obstreperously and emphatically global."[74] Kwame Appiah, however, adopts a utopian view. By Appiah's reckoning, one of the consequences of globalization is the receding of the nation state as a moral community, but a community that needs to be defended and reconstructed, not just at the level of the nation but also at the local level, "the town, the street, the business, the craft, the family," for example.[75] In an argument that agrees with Doreen Massey's "ethics of place" and Bahira Trask's ethical perspective on modern families, Appiah nicely describes the cultural place of the family as a "'near sphere' of moral concern."[76] In Appiah's analysis, the family is one among other natural and appropriate venues for symbolic discussions about ethics in an age of "rooted cosmopolitanism" that can balance obligations to local and global communities.

Time will tell whether the generational family drama can adapt to shifting social conditions, but in the meantime, new dramas are emerging that are motivated by a desire for social justice on a more global stage, and which propose ethical relationships with more distant strangers. They are continuous with the tradition of the generational family drama – and are accordingly sometimes framed in public discourse as multicultural – but in these new dramas, the stranger has broken out of the domestic sphere to become itinerant or distant, a subject of potential sympathy and compassion – an object of seeing, knowing, and caring. What this has meant is that some of the material, social conditions that have, as I have argued in this chapter, been absented are again made visible and available to critique. It is a theatre explicitly concerned not with the reaffirmation or inclusion of any particular community in the multicultural nation but theatre with a global ethics. The following chapter explores how theatre's growing interest in global ethics is producing a different theatrical poetics.

4

A New Melodrama of Globalization

When we produce narratives of "anonymous corporeality and speechlessness," when we hide our own implication and stand outside of history, preoccupied with our own pain, we stake out the colour line, producing ourselves as individuals and as a nation on the civilized side of things. In this we have not been alone, although the position of "trauma damaged idealist" has suited our middle-power aspirations to a T.

Sherene Razack, *Dark Threats and White Knights*[1]

Rahul Varma's play *Bhopal* offers a dramatic account of an infamous 1984 industrial accident in Bhopal, India, at the Union Carbide chemical factory in which a release of toxic gas resulted in the immediate deaths of ten thousand people and the injury of many more over the long term. Varma's play – which features only one character based on a historical figure, Union Carbide CEO Warren Anderson – is an emotionally charged drama about a Canadian researcher, Dr Sonya Labonté, who travels to Bhopal to research the disaster and is met with fierce resistance from Union Carbide officials and Indian politicians. The play's own trajectory echoes the journey of its protagonist; it was produced first in 2001 in Montreal at the Teesri Duniya Theatre in the immediate aftermath of 9/11; at Toronto's Theatre Centre in 2003; later reprised in Montreal in 2014; and then taken to Chennai, India, in 2016.

Bhopal is an example of a growing number of Canadian plays that deal with global issues and stage distant strangers, which I mean here to refer to people outside the country, as well as, by implication, those who are not members of some shared community – of nation, of culture, of race. This is a different notion of the stranger from the one I have used in the previous chapters, where the strangers discussed were first- and second-generation Canadians. The distant stranger occupies a position not just at the threshold of local or national communities but at the threshold of the human community, somehow excluded or left behind by global modernity. It was my observation that such distant strangers were appearing in Canadian theatre with greater frequency that initially inspired me to write this book. In this chapter, I describe the poetics of these plays as a kind of "new melodrama of globalization" and offer it as one prominent example of Paul Rae's "[stories] the first world is telling itself about globalization."[2] Rae's phrase is especially apt because of its suggestion that a focus on the distant stranger is what enables a story to be told about and to the self by way of audiences to Canadian theatre. As Sherene Razack makes clear in the passage quoted in the epigraph, a story may construct a "we" who sits too comfortably on the "civilized side of things." The new melodrama of globalization tries to disturb any easy or comforting relationship to distant strangers but, I argue, its strategies for doing so may reproduce a moralism haunted by the very colonialism it sets out to critique. At stake is the merit of a popular mode of engaging with global issues and, by extension, the value of theatre as a cultural medium for engaging with the urgent geopolitical issues of the moment.

A key trope within the new melodrama of globalization is the "journey narrative," in which a character embarks on a humanitarian quest to "help" the distant stranger. The plays mentioned at the end of the previous chapter were each structured around journeys – to the Philippines in *Every Letter Counts* and Bosnia in *RETURN*. The plays I discuss here – Varma's *Bhopal*, Ahmed Ghazali's *The Sheep and the Whale*, and Matthew Mackenzie's *SIA* – also feature a journey narrative, and there are many others besides.[3] Just as the generational family drama emerged in Canadian theatre as a popular dramaturgical container for stories of migration and cultural identity, journey narratives are ubiquitous in a new melodrama of globalization. While the distant strangers of this chapter are different people than the strangers of the previous chapters, these melodramas similarly position them as objects of fetishization or ejection from a community of the "we" constructed by the performance, victims this time not of misunderstanding or prejudice but of the dehumanizing consequences of aggressive capitalism and neoliberal globalization.

Haunted as they are by a long history of colonial and ethnographic quests into the "unknown," journey narratives demand critical attention. In the spirit of Razack's critique of Canadian peacekeeping narratives, it seems relevant to ask how an audience, and by extension the public, is configured in "our" journey to "discover" or "help" distant strangers. The most troubling form of the journey narrative is the "white knight" story, in which a Western, usually white, and often male, character travels to encounter strangers in another part of the world, perpetuating what Razack calls a "politics of rescue."[4] If it was the case that the generational family drama threatened to domesticate strangers by collapsing their experience into a satisfying personal self-fulfillment, then it may be even more concerning to collapse it further into an individual's story of confrontation with difference, where the movement is not toward reconciliation with family, or with a "community" or "culture," but toward an even more individualized epiphany. Looking through the theatrical lenses of *Bhopal*, *The Sheep and the Whale*, and *SIA*, I want to explore how audiences of the new melodrama of globalization are configured in a global ethics of care for distant strangers.

BHOPAL AND A NEW MELODRAMA OF GLOBALIZATION

When *NOW Magazine* theatre critic Glen Sumi offhandedly remarked that some elements of *Bhopal* were "melodramatic,"[5] and other critics disparaged it as a "Movie of the Week Gone Wrong,"[6] with "stick figure" characters and "soap opera tangents,"[7] they glimpsed that *Bhopal* is an example of what I would suggest is a new melodrama of globalization that echoes and reinvents the features of historical stage melodramas. The fact that these comments invoke melodrama as an *aesthetic* criticism (as breaches in its otherwise naturalistic style) rather than as a *moral* one (that it prescribes meaning to its audience) is telling of the extent to which a moral mode melodrama has become normalized in Canadian theatre that deals with global issues.

"Melodrama" is a complex term that applies to many historical and contemporary cultural forms and which has, as theatre historian Jonas Barish has pointed out, taken on pejorative connotations to become an example of "anti-theatrical prejudice," a suspicion of theatricality itself.[8] Melodrama is familiar to many people today largely by way of its popularity in American film, but its features were established in novels and on the stage nearly a century before film appeared. Peter Brooks's definitive study of nineteenth-century melodrama, *The Melodramatic Imagination,* offers a rich portrait of the form's roots and characteristics, particularly in France.[9] In the nineteenth century melodrama was so successful that Brooks discusses it not as a literary genre but as a widespread cultural "imagination," a general "pervasive melodramatism" that circulated in Western Europe in the period.[10] The fundamental motivation of melodrama, and the source of its satisfaction for audiences, is its expression of a clear moral order in a world otherwise lacking transcendent certainty. As Brooks writes, it is "an intense emotional and ethical drama based on the manichaeistic struggle of good and evil, a world where what one lives for and by is seen in terms of, and as determined by, the most fundamental psychic relations and cosmic ethical forces."[11] Similarly, Ben Singer notes in his book *Melodrama and Modernity* that melodrama "served a quasi-religious ameliorative function in reassuring audiences that a higher cosmic moral force still looked down on the world and governed it with an ultimately just hand."[12] Melodrama assures its audiences that, whatever the ubiquity of injustice, there remains a transcendent and durable moral structure struggling to prevail.

Bhopal exhibits many of the features of nineteenth-century melodrama, which Brooks identifies as: "[the] indulgence of strong emotionalism; moral polarization and schematization; extreme states of being, situations, actions; overt villainy; persecution of the good and final reward of virtue; inflated and extravagant expression; dark plotting, suspense [and] breathtaking peripety."[13] In the first place, *Bhopal*'s targets are closely reminiscent of those of nineteenth-century melodrama: social and economic inequality, ineffectual politicians, exploitative capitalists, and abusive factory owners. The play exhibits strong emotionalism and its moral polarization is crystal clear. One of the distant strangers in the play is Bhopal resident Izzat, described in promotional materials for the play as a "destitute slum dweller" who has a visibly disabled child as a consequence of the accident. The wittingly cruel villain, Union Carbide CEO Warren Anderson, has his henchman in India, Union Carbide plant boss Devraj, lobby for an Orwellian "People's Progress Zone" around the plant that will be free of regulation in the lead-up to the disaster. Dr Labonté is a virtuous researcher on a messianic quest to expose the environmental and physical consequences of the disaster. When two politicians – Indian minister Jaganlal and Canadian ambassador Sauvé – collude with Anderson to thwart the doctor's work, the evil is complete; at one point, Sauvé even discourages Dr Labonté from helping a choking resident of the slums because doing so will make her "legally responsible."[14] The play leans heavily on Brooks's "breaktaking peripety," with dramatic and sudden reversals in the action precipitated by dramatic events, including what was referred to in historical melodrama as a "sensation scene," the spectacular event of the explosion of the factory itself that precipitates Minister Jaganlal's change of heart and has him rescue Dr Labonté from exile. Similarly lifted from a nineteenth-century melodrama is a subplot involving the villain's secretary Madiha, who is revealed to be pregnant with her boss's child. Initially supporting her boss and lover, Madiha is knocked unconscious and poisoned in the explosion of the factory, loses her baby, and like Jaganlal, turns against Union Carbide. Madiha is an example of the "detective" figure in historical melodrama, a secondary character – sometimes the villain's servant just as in Varma's play – who, seized by a sudden pang of conscientiousness, switches sides to undo the treachery. Madiha is set to fly out of India with the cowardly Devraj but, in the play's final climactic reversal, tears up her plane ticket and moves to hold the hand of the victim Izzat. The play's ending – "*The women have resolute expressions of defiance. The End.*"[15] – offers the satisfaction of what James Leslie Smith calls a "melodrama of triumph," in which a character is seen, despite terrifically difficult circumstances, to attain a moral victory.[16] By the play's end Dr Labonté is reduced to obscurity but she perseveres in her work. The vector of the audience's sympathies in the play is clear: their narrative guide is the white knight doctor, the victim is the distant stranger "slum dweller," and no matter the outcome, as in all melodrama, it is the moral rather than the material victory that matters. Villainy is not overcome but outwitted, goodness not established but acknowledged.

That *Bhopal* would exhibit features of a dramatic form established in the nineteenth century is not surprising. If the class warfare and inequality of the nineteenth century proved fertile soil for melodrama, then the high levels of social and economic inequality of twenty-first-century neoliberal capitalism have again fertilized that soil. In his influential book *Capital in the Twenty-First Century* French economist Thomas Piketty uses new data and methods to argue that levels of income inequality today have regressed to levels not observed since the nineteenth century following a period of relative equalizing.[17] It is this iteration of social anxieties that Zygmunt Bauman elucidates in his book *Collateral Damage*. The "endemic or contrived invisibility of collateral 'victims' of a liquid modern world," he says, "have made the world's poorest people expendable."[18] As the examples to come in this chapter better illustrate, however, there is something new about how melodrama features in these stories about globalization. While historical melodrama had to delineate a world of heroes and villains, the new melodrama of globalization offers a more self-conscious morality. Melodrama, Brooks writes, "comes into being in a world where the traditional imperatives of truth and ethics have been violently thrown into question, yet where the promulgation of truth and ethics, their instauration as a way of life, is of immediate, daily, political concern."[19] At least in its realizations in Canadian theatre, melodrama rarely names the "good" and "bad" unequivocally but instead reveals "a set of ethical imperatives to be made clear."[20] This is why it is often the case that the journey narratives featured in this theatre fail in their humanitarian quests; their actual purpose is not to succeed but to make available a clear moral order.

What also seems urgent in the new melodrama of globalization is a desire for visibility. Depicting a world in which the forces of injustice and its most vulnerable victims are occulted from public view, the new form takes advantage of the highly visual medium of theatre to somehow restore these to visibility. This aim has an interesting precedent in a feature of historical melodrama that Brooks identifies: what he calls a "desire to speak all," a tendency to over-explain the action, to talk out the conflict. The desire to "speak all," Brooks suggests, exists in tension with a simultaneous obsession with an ineffable terror often featured in melodramatic narratives, realized, for example, in characters who stand stupefied and speechless in the face of a threat.[21] In the nineteenth century, the stupefying spectacle was typically a nightmare vision of the industrial age, the fragile human figure facing annihilation by a terrible machine, as in the iconic trope of the freight train bearing down on a victim tied to the tracks. The new melodrama of globalization features moments of the same stupefied paralysis upon bearing witness to a terrible human catastrophe.

STRANGERS AT A DISTANCE

In the previous chapters, I showed how first- and second-generation immigrants, represented as strangers on the Canadian stage, anticipated specific kinds of seeing and knowing in their audiences. In this chapter I look at how audiences may be placed in a relationship of *care* for distant strangers. The question of how we experience empathy or compassion at a distance has long been at issue in philosophy. Hannah Arendt argued in *On Revolution* that compassion is a noble quality when experienced in relationship with a specific person, in a face-to-face relationship.[22] For Arendt, it was the specificity of that relationship that made it actionable. When, by contrast, compassion is requested for a generalized other, it becomes "eloquent" and "loquacious," offering only an immobilizing pity. Compassion, she suggests, is a principle on which to act, whereas pity "recognizes and discovers itself as emotion and feeling."[23] Agreeing with Arendt, the French sociologist Luc Boltanski draws on psychological research to support the notion that we are more strongly disposed to help someone when that relationship has been made particular (and think as well of the lesson of Philippa Foot's famous "trolley" thought experiment in philosophy, discussed at length by Kwame Appiah in *Experiments in Ethics*[24]). Boltanski asks, "Why else present a spectacle of suffering human beings to unconcerned people if not to draw their attention to it and so direct them to action?"[25] In the end, one is left with the fatalism that, as Boltanski puts it, "the whole pity relationship requires distance, [that] if they were 'here,' we wouldn't pity them anymore."[26] The problem had even been observed by Georg Simmel in his nineteenth-century essay about the stranger, in which he observed that "the more distant the stranger the more general the qualities that are in common with them," adding, in his terms, a "coolness" to the relation.[27]

Our relationship to distant strangers is precisely the focus of Moroccan-Canadian Ahmed Ghazali's play *The Sheep and the Whale* (hereafter, *Sheep*), first produced in Montreal in French in 2001 and in a translation by Bobby Theodore in Toronto in 2007. Both continuous with the generational family drama and representative of a theatre more urgently and explicitly concerned with global ethics and the relationship to distant strangers, *Sheep* deals with the problem of illegal migration. Set on a cargo ship adrift on the Strait of Gibraltar – a threshold space in many senses – the play immediately announces its concern with global ethics by means of its stage directions: "The stage is an old, worn down, and poorly maintained Russian cargo ship. It is also the world, or our Earth which is also just as wrecked."[28] It opens with a human catastrophe: a boat carrying refugees fleeing Africa has capsized near the ship and the ship's crew is frantically pulling the bodies of the dead – and one lone survivor – aboard in the midst of a storm. The ship's captain, inconvenienced rather than horrified, spends much of the play trying to convince port authorities in Gibraltar (Europe) and Tangiers (Africa) to accept the bodies without making him pay port-taxes; Gibraltar refuses because they do not want any more African refugees to deal with, and Tangiers because the incident has coincided with Aid al-Adha, a Muslim holiday of sacrifice. At the same time, an African stowaway on the ship evades the capture of the ship's ruthless crew, and garners some sympathy from the ship's doctor. All of this is overseen – in some scenes literally, from an upper deck onstage – by a couple, Hélène, who is French, and Hassan, who is Arab-Moroccan. The couple had boarded the ship to go to the Canary Islands for a vacation, but the catastrophe precipitates a fracture in their relationship that sends them on divergent journeys – Hélène toward a confrontation with her own Western privilege, and Hassan on an ancestral journey back "home" to Morocco.

Sheep grafts a generational family drama onto a melodrama of globalization. Much like the characters in the plays discussed in chapter 3, Hassan is visited and haunted by the life he lived prior to his emigration, pestered by visions that drag him into the depths of a troubled psyche from which he must release himself in order to be remade. He is on an ancestral journey back to the Africa of his youth, a life he had traded for his life in Paris, and as the ship drifts toward Morocco in the play, he begins to pick up an Arabic accent in English (or French in the original production) and to speak involuntarily in Arabic as though being repossessed by his former and "authentic" self. As in some of the generational family dramas, the culture to which Hassan is drawn is represented as a "primordial" one of myth and ritual that makes a spectral appearance in the character's dreams or repressed memory – the cultural "other" repressed in the modern subject. One of the play's expressionistic dream sequences, for instance, has Hassan imagining he is participating in an Aid al-Adha ritual of cutting a ram's throat in a sacrificial feast. The act becomes a test of Hassan's true identity – his validation as a Moroccan depending on his ability to perform his role in the ritual. When he balks, a chorus of revellers grabs his hands and forces them to the ram's throat. Hassan collapses at the sight of the blood, and then, seemingly possessed by the spirit, enters a trance, dances, collapses onto the body of the ram, and awakes to discover that he has been lying among the dead stowaways on the ship's deck. Just as with personal revelations in the earlier plays, the vision impels Hassan to reconcile his two worlds, which for him means revealing to Hélène that he did not immigrate to France years earlier but went there himself as an illegal stowaway though Spain. In the end, now unburdened of the "lie" he had been living in France, Hassan "accidentally" drops his French passport overboard, and "throws his bag over his shoulders and goes down the ramp and disappears into Tangiers,"[29] his transformation complete.

Onto this familiar dramaturgy, *Sheep* grafts another one that is explicitly concerned with the ethical relationship to distant strangers.[30] The play offers a discourse on the idea of ethical witnessing that is doubled when realized for a public audience onstage; witnessing contains possibilities for knowing, recognizing, or caring for distant strangers. The play is especially invested in a kind of responsible seeing, a seeing that should become self-conscious and attached to an additional obligation. Ghazali's apprehension about how an audience might witness poorly is realized through one of the play's two white-knight characters, Hélène, whose attempt to confront the situation proves disastrous. Hélène professes to be a cosmopolitan woman sympathetic to the stowaways of the play, but she recoils in horror from what she sees, turns her eyes away at several points, and reprimands Hassan for depriving her of the sanitized experience of a romantic vacation. At the start of the play, when the bodies are being plucked from the water, Hélène "silently watches what is unfolding from the upper deck,"[31] and says of her own paralysis: "It was awful! I saw them drown, there were so many, Hassan, the waves sucked them under like bugs, there was nothing we could do, the waves, the storm, there was nothing anyone could do."[32] Her inability to intervene – "They must have alerted the Red Cross or the UN. The rescue teams are on their way … Don't panic!"[33] – is itself a set piece in historical stage melodramas – the delayed rescue. Desperate to shake Hélène from her willed ignorance, Hassan forces her to look at the dead bodies and acknowledge their specificity: "Look at this one; he's a Berber. I can tell from the colour of his eyes. This one is an Arab … Closer! Don't worry they aren't rotting yet. Salted as they are, they'll stay preserved longer."[34] The act of forced looking bizarrely becomes an act of forced sex when Hassan and Hélène retreat into the shadows and Hassan conjures up a litany of strangers from all around the world (he lists fifty-one nationalities) who encircle Hélène and tear her clothes from her body, sexualizing the political and cultural threat they have already represented in the play.[35] Hélène's bearing witness to the horror is more than disempowering; it is destructive. At the end of the play, in a moment reminiscent of melodrama's strong emotionalism, Hélène is seen "curled up into a ball in a dark corner on the upper deck. She is crying bitterly."[36] The moment presents the distant strangers of the play as shadowy and monstrous, expressionistic projections of an ancient Western fear and anxiety about being overwhelmed by strangers, a fear justified by their violent sexual aggression. Whatever the audience is to make of the troubling moment, the distant strangers become a threatening mob, a trope to which I return in the Epilogue as an instance of a contemporary "stranger danger."

In keeping with Arendt's and Boltanski's notions that care for strangers is contingent on specificity, there is a sense in *Sheep* that to apprehend the distant strangers' specificity, to even hear their "story," is to enter into a relationship of care with them. Indeed, a new melodrama of globalization might generally be equipped to give the distant stranger a face or voice, an identity and a meaningful relationship to an audience. As in the example of Hélène's encounter with a mob of strangers described above, however, the trouble is that the interlocutors – the journeying characters – become more "humanized"

4.1 Julian Richings as the Doctor (right) and Karim Morgan as the Stowaway (left) in the Cahoots Theatre Company and Modern Times Stage Company's 2007 production of Ahmed Ghazali's *The Sheep and the Whale*.

than the distant strangers. Focus falls on the impact on the witness, while those presented as "victims" are abstracted and dehistoricized. This is particularly true of perhaps the most clear theatricalization of the stranger onstage discussed in this book. The Stowaway in *Sheep*, a black African character hiding on the cargo ship who is hunted by the ship's villainous crew, makes only a couple of appearances in the shadows, a stranger at the threshold of the human community in any sense. At one point, the Doctor recalls to Hassan a conversation he had with the Stowaway, at which point, in the Theatre Passe Muraille production, Karim Morgan as the Stowaway slowly walked to the front of the stage with eyes transfixed on the horizon, his clothes in tatters and his feet in slave chains:

THE DOCTOR: Tell me where you're from.
THE STOWAWAY: From Africa.
THE DOCTOR: Which country?
THE STOWAWAY: A poor country.

THE DOCTOR: Which one?
THE STOWAWAY: A burning country.
THE DOCTOR: Which one?
THE STOWAWAY: I don't have a country, or maybe I forgot.[37]

The Stowaway – a nightmare vision of the generational family drama – is uprooted and orphaned by a forgotten and unrecoverable ancestry. Milija Gluhovic, in his own commentary on *Sheep*, draws on philosopher Giorgio Agamben's notion of the "bare life" to see the Stowaway as a generalized portrait of the refugee who must be stripped of individualism, perhaps as a first step toward perpetuating an inconsequential violence, perhaps as a first step toward fitting into a new context.[38] The witness to the spectacle is rendered inarticulate and immobile (perhaps a theatricalization of Kwame Appiah's multicultural "Medusa Syndrome" that would petrify identity?[39]). At such moments, language as a container of meaning seems to break down and the tragic is experienced mainly through its embodied presence. This is a contradiction inherent in melodramatic representation; in spite of its desire to speak all, it becomes silent at the brink of an ineffable terror. By refusing to become any specific stowaway under the Doctor's questioning and gaze, the Stowaway refuses a responsible looking that would lead to knowing or caring, standing instead, as in historical melodrama, "stupefied" by the spectacle of the stranger. The Doctor wants to care, wants a story, but cannot get one. The focus is thrown back on the validity of his questions and the integrity of his compassion.

Julie Salverson has written about a kind of "erotics of injury" in some theatre about experiences of trauma. Her concern is about the kind of ethics that theatre occasions. "If we write a play that presents an uncomplicated portrayal of victims, villains, and heroes," she asks, "what choices do we give an audience about how to relate?"[40] Salverson identifies "testimony" and "witness" as key features of theatre that deals with the "tragic other," and she offers an illustration from a college performance she had seen that a group of students had devised from children's stories from the Bosnian war:

> What disturbed me was a sense that the students were not present in the performance, were not noticing themselves in the picture,

> and, consequently, that we as audience members were neither asked nor were able to implicate ourselves. Audience and actors together were looking out at some exoticized and deliberately tragic other. Even more discomforting than the voyeurism I felt a participant in was the almost erotic manner in which the actors performed pain. Several audience members expressed being extremely moved by the whole thing. But what, I wondered, was our obligation as witnesses to this story, to this unacknowledged pleasure? Yes, the audience was moved, but by and toward what?[41]

Salverson noticed that, despite the overtly "ethical" content of the performance, the audience seemed expected to respond in a prescribed way to the exoticized and eroticized pain – in the manner, I would suggest, of the "moral" mode of performance I outlined in the first chapter.[42]

Sheep similarly cues the audience to respond in an expected fashion. The Stowaway is a distant stranger at the threshold between worlds, literally a desperate migrant, and performatively a figure abstracted but nonetheless present in Karim Morgan's gripping performance of the role in the Theatre Passe Muraille production. But the Doctor's reaction to him, and inevitably, by extension, the audience's, sinks into what Arendt calls an "immobilizing pity." The "collateral victims" of the play's story never get a story of their own, the Stowaway is emptied of history and memory, and the lone survivor from the capsized boat jumps overboard before his story is told. The still and silent bodies of the refugees lie on the stage for the entire play, animated only for the sacrificial ritual.[43] The play is rigidly schematized into light and dark dramatic worlds and the distant stranger is set in an unreachable position in the latter, the imagery and dialogue mapping out a familiar pattern of the global north as civilized and progressive, and the global south as a place of darkness, fear, and ignorance. This scheme is first coded into the set, where the deck becomes the public place of visibility and interaction, and the cargo containers form a shadowy and menacing world – in Ghazali's words, "a labyrinth of corridors and dark and narrow passageways that make the audience feel uncomfortable and help them to imagine that many things can happen in this dark place that is The South, Africa, the jungle, the north of Paris, the ghetto."[44] The play divides the world according to a long-established colonial pattern that associates Europe with intellect and civilization and Africa with passion and sexuality. As the Stowaway says: "I can't stay in the South because I won't have a memory and I can't stay in the North because I won't have a heart … That's why here, halfway between North and South, I'm more fragile than a spider web, because I don't have either a heart or a memory."[45] The image was picked up on in a postcard promotion of the play that showed the outlines of the Strait of Gibraltar with a brain superimposed over Spain, and a heart over Morocco.[46]

In spite of the melodramatic poetics, *Sheep* is clearly intent on provoking its audience to think more deeply about how "we" see, know, or care for distant strangers. *Sheep* invites its viewers to face a critically important central dilemma of global ethics: what is our responsibility to distant strangers? As Peter Singer asks in *One World*, if people do feel an ethical obligation to those around them, what are the ethical, social, or political mechanisms that break down when the ethical community is extended to the globe? *Sheep* exhibits genuine passion and goodwill in wrestling with this problem, and Ghazali is clearly conscious of it. Reflecting on a playwriting workshop he had conducted in Barcelona, several years after *Sheep* was written and produced, Ghazali noted the need to avoid "imposing ethnocentric views, thereby renewing anthropological literature and travel novels that have been associated with Western colonialism."[47] Brooks said of historical melodrama that it is not about the triumph of good, particularly because the good is typically broken, defeated, and sentenced to obscurity and invisibility by the end of the drama – in just the way Hassan is at the end of *Sheep*. Despite that defeat, or perhaps because of it, melodrama is about "the admiration of virtue," which is only made more admirable by its failure.[48] Melodramas paint the world in high contrast, whatever the outcomes, and they gift a "moral legibility" to their audiences, "spelling out its ethical forces and imperatives in large and bold characters."[49] The disappointment of *Sheep*, however, is that it fails to translate the impulse toward compassion for distant strangers into a poetics that is ethically engaging for its audience, and the play seems even resigned to the conclusion that responsible looking is out of reach. The characters who react compassionately to the tragedy at the heart of the story – Hélène, the Doctor, and Hassan – all have failed encounters with strangers. Hélène does everything she can to deny and look away, clinging to the naïve notion that these distant strangers must have someone taking care of them, and that surely she can't be expected to do anything; when the distant stranger suddenly becomes present and "real," and an "out there" becomes a "here," Hélène is shattered by the threat that she had previously been able to compartmentalize. We know the Doctor is the principled one, the voice of right moral action in the play, but we expect that he too must suffer for his idealism, and indeed, by the end of the play he seems to abandon his vocation. Hassan presents some balance between these two, but his solution – to disappear into Tangiers – is the expected conclusion to the generational family drama but an unsatisfying end in terms of the play's ostensible goal of forging a meaningful relationship with distant strangers. In the tradition of melodrama, *Sheep* offers a moral legibility of "us" and "them" and some self-consciousness about the implications of the audience's looking; but, in producing what Razack called "narratives of anonymous corporeality and speechlessness," it is ultimately more moral than ethical.

DARK THREATS, WHITE KNIGHTS

Comparisons were inevitable when two performances on a common subject, one with an enormous global audience and the other with a small and local audience, took place within weeks of one another in March 2012. The first to appear was *KONY 2012*, a slick, half-hour activist video created by the American charity Invisible Children and narrated by its co-founder Jason Russell. It immediately went viral and has since accumulated 100 million views on YouTube.[50] Two weeks after that video first appeared, Cahoots Theatre Company opened Matthew MacKenzie's play *SIA* at the Factory Theatre in Toronto. Both *KONY 2012* and *SIA* highlight the brutal campaigns of violence and recruitment of child soldiers by Central African warlords – in *KONY 2012* by the still at-large Ugandan warlord Joseph Kony and in *SIA* by a semi-fictional "Butcher of Liberia" suggestive of ex-Liberian dictator Charles Taylor. Russell and MacKenzie both travelled to Central Africa to research their projects, and their respective narratives foreground their own processes of journey and encounter.

And both pieces were criticized, albeit on vastly different scales, leading Martin Morrow at the time to comment in the *Globe and Mail*, "it's been a rough month for well-meaning white guys." [51] A great deal differentiates *SIA* from *KONY 2012*, however. *KONY 2012* was part of an activist campaign prescribing specific actions its viewers might take to – in its own controversial language – "Make Kony Famous," encouraging viewers, on a designated day dubbed "Cover the Night," to write messages on social media and put up posters in their communities to make Joseph Kony as publicly "visible" as possible, so as to increase pressure on Western governments to support the Ugandan effort to find and arrest him. *SIA* also aimed to bring the atrocities of a warlord to "visibility" but hoped as well to stimulate a more thoughtful engagement with the ethics of Western intervention in the issue. I don't intend to compare these differently situated performances here, but *KONY 2012* provides a useful backdrop to consider what the journey narrative means for staging distant strangers in each piece.

The prevalence of journey narratives makes them one clear answer to Paul Rae's question about what kinds of stories the first world is telling itself about globalization. In Nina Lee Aquino's *Every Letter Counts* and Theatrefront's *RETURN: The Sarajevo Project*, characters go on ancestral journeys to confront their familial and cultural histories; in *Bhopal*, Dr Labonté travels to India to bring corrupt industrialists to justice; in *Sheep*, both Hélène and the Doctor are on a mission to expose the crew's transgressions and to see and know the stowaways; and both *KONY 2012* and *SIA* are structured around a humanitarian journey to Africa.[52] These journey stories are a new spin on an old – even ancient – trope, stretching back to one of the oldest extant stories in the Western tradition – Gilgamesh's journey to Cedar Mountain in the three-millennia-old Sumerian folktale, *The Epic of Gilgamesh*. Journeys featured especially prominently in the travel literature of the eighteenth and nineteenth centuries, where they were intertwined with the foundational work in anthropology. Mary Louise Pratt has written about how that tradition of travel literature helped produce "the rest of the world" for European readers. "Tales of journeys," she writes, "produced a Eurocentered form of global [or] planetary consciousness."[53]

The connection between the journey narrative and melodrama is illuminated by Sherene Razack's book *Dark Threats and White Knights*. Razack looks at how the Rwandan genocide of 1994 was narrated in public discourse by Roméo Dallaire, the major-general of the United Nations Mission for Rwanda at the time. Like Jason Russell, Dallaire positioned himself in the Canadian public consciousness as the primary witnessing subject of the otherwise "invisible" victims of the genocide. Razack is especially interested in the narrative and visual strategies of *Witness the Evil*, a documentary in which Dallaire speaks in melodramatic terms about having encountered "the devil" in Rwanda. Razack notes how over time Dallaire himself became the psychologically damaged victim of the narrative, thereby relegating the actual, anonymous, faceless victims to the background. "We come to know of the Rwandan genocide as a horror that is unknowable and unthinkable," she writes. "The 'flood of terrifying images' tells us all we need to know, and in place of history and context, the very information needed to consider the future."[54] But more concerning than the absenting of nuanced information about the genocide is the way this narrative constitutes its viewing subject: "*Witness the Evil* and the news features on Dallaire invite us to understand ourselves racially as well as nationally – that is, as good people forced to stand helplessly by as evil unfolds and as more powerful nations refuse to help."[55]

Razack thus points the way to a discussion not of how the journey narrative conceives of the distant stranger, but of how it conceives of those who encounter the stranger. This matters, because discourse around journeys often situates the stranger in either moral or pedagogical terms. Michael Hardt and Antonio Negri, in their analysis of "Empire," the term they use to describe a new global "juridical order," link journey narratives to a moral and political ideology that seeks to justify Western interventionism. "Contrary to the way many postmodernist accounts would have it," they write, "the imperial machine, far from eliminating master narratives, actually produces and reproduces them (ideological master narratives in particular) in order to validate and celebrate its own power."[56] In other words, moral quests into ethically vacant barrens become Empire's means of policing its borders, and Hardt and Negri put NGO activities such as those of Invisible Children at the core of this process. Through their lens, *KONY 2012* looks like a means for a culture to publicly denounce its sinners ("or rather the Enemy in properly inquisitorial terms"[57]), such that its "moral intervention … becomes a frontline force of imperial intervention."[58] In one gesture, the white knight reveals evil trespasses and reproduces an ideology of Empire.

KONY 2012 is, unabashedly and by design, a melodramatic white knight narrative. MacKenzie's play *SIA*, on the other hand, warrants a closer analysis. In MacKenzie's play, the journeying character is Nick Summers, a young, male, white Canadian who travels to Accra, Ghana, to volunteer in a refugee camp. In the play's precipitating incident, Nick befriends a man named Saa Wonleh, who protects him in a scuffle at a nightclub. After Nick passes out and wakes up in the morning, however, he discovers that his new friend is his kidnapper. Two stories unfold in parallel in the play: one set in the present in which Saa tortures Nick and tries to extort money from his family back in Canada; another set in the past in which we see Saa mentoring his younger sister Sia. The mystery of the play is: what has changed Saa the responsible role model into Saa the desperate and drug-addicted kidnapper? The answer, we eventually learn, is that he was forced into being a child soldier in his youth, forced by militia men even to kill his own father. Saa's motivation to kidnap Nick is revealed to be a desperate attempt to prevent his sister from having to testify at a war crimes tribunal against the Butcher of Liberia. It doesn't pan out as he had planned, and, as the police close in on him, Saa is faced with the decision to kill them both or surrender to authorities.

SIA wades into ethical waters that are not within sight in *KONY 2012*.[59] In contrast to *KONY 2012*, and to a more straightforward melodrama such as *Bhopal*, *SIA* offers its audience an unreliable narrator. From the play's opening moments, Nick is a troubled and troubling guide, a hedonist whose intentions are immediately in doubt. In fact the plot involves two morally compromised characters: Nick, an unlikable white knight motivated by an admirable desire to "help," and Saa, a kidnapper and torturer whom the audience is asked to understand differently when it learns of his recruitment as a child soldier who was forced, as in Kony's practice, to prove his mettle by murdering his own kin. At issue, as Saa and Nick argue their way through their tense standoff, is the merit of Nick's journey to Ghana, and along with it, writ large, the merit of Western interventionism in such complex situations. In his arrogance, Nick takes the length of the play to realize that his trip to Ghana was self-interested and futile: "I wanted to help," he acknowledges, "but I don't know what I'm helping, I don't know who I'm helping – no – I'm helping myself, I came here for myself, that is what's true. I haven't done anything. Nothing."[60] Nick's ultimate willingness to question the journey creates a space in which the terms of engagement with the distant stranger are opened for negotiation, and the audience is made aware, through the way the play has been framed, that such questions extend to the playwright himself, who researched the play by taking his own journey first to a Liberian refugee camp in Ghana (like the one in which the play is set) and later to do a workshop in Monrovia, Liberia, with artists from the Liberian Dance Troupe. MacKenzie's impulse to structure his own journey of discovery was realized not only in the play but also on Cahoots Theatre Company's blog, to which he posted a seven-minute video serving as a documentary "trailer" for the show.[61] Even though the play tells a fictional story, MacKenzie's choices place an interpretive frame around the piece as his own working through of his journey and encounter with difference in Africa. Here, the notion of an "artists's journey" as a creative process mixes with the white knight's journey into the unknown, offering its audience an additional axis of identification with the play.

Yet, to pose a challenging question to *SIA*: how is the audience being asked to see, know, or care about its distant strangers in such a self-aware and ethically conscious drama? Salverson provides a further angle for critique when she questions the "authenticity" to which "testimonial" theatre appeals. In these narratives, pain and trauma are taken to be the sole, or at least primary, marker of the "authentic" experience of the suffering of distant strangers. Consequently, strangers become a tragic absence or loss, to the exclusion of other theatrical dimensions such as humour or imagination. Also, to fuse the arguments of Razack and Salverson, the tragic other authenticates the white knight's experience, leading to a situation in which "telling one's story" constitutes its own ethical justification, and the authenticity of witness becomes a rightness of witness. Russell provided a notable instance of this justification when, after being challenged in an interview by Jian Ghomeshi on CBC Radio's program *Q* about why he featured himself so prominently in *KONY 2012*, he replied that he didn't intend to become a "celebrity" himself but wanted to tell "an honest and vulnerable story."[62] Ghomeshi had asked Russell to justify the white knight story, and in his response, drawing on a discourse of authenticity, Russell presented himself as the victim of the public's gawking (a public relations strategy that his interviewer would himself later put to use). "I'm still proud of putting myself in the *KONY 2012* video," Russell offered; "I knew I had to authentically share my story."[63] If the journey narrative shifted the focus away from the victims, the discourse of the artist's "authentic" meta-theatrical encounter with the other only further separated the discourse from a discussion of context and system and geopolitical implications, placing it instead in interpersonal relations and investments, and rehearsing what Terry Eagleton has called the "customary Western vice" of thinking of the other in terms of the self.[64]

While Salverson's focus on representing the pain and injury of victims addresses the audience, Razack offers a way to think as well about how the heroes address the audience, a "melodramatic poetics of rescue," complementing Salverson's "erotics of injury." Despite the fact that white knights are possessed of doubt, and also *because* they are, their journey positions them in a stance of moral enlightenment and responsibility for the distant stranger. Such dramas, Razack writes, invite the viewer "into the 'abstracted space of universalizing authority over others' [and] to join a fraternity ... of those who are neither of the hacked bodies on an African landscape nor of the unscrupulous United States or incompetent UN." And before long, he adds, "we begin to feel the bond that comes from sharing such high moral ground."[65] In just the way Robert L. King suggested that theatre sometimes "flattens" its audience into a position of moral authority (discussed in chapter 1), the journey may invite the audience to admire its own collective virtue. Here we find the reappearance of a problem that has surfaced in other ways in previous chapters; audiences to a Multicultural Theatre Festival or a generational family drama, for instance, could be satisfied in their own gesture of "welcoming" the stranger into some imagined community by virtue, before anything else, of their having attended these performances. Consequently, strangers may remain distant, and the audience's act of witness does little more, as Jacqueline Lo and Helen Gilbert have provocatively put it, than to allow the audience to "publicly enact its shame."[66]

To avoid that hazard, the representation must find a way to refuse the audience this position of superiority, both in a challenge to Western interventionism and in an effort to create a more meaningful ethical encounter with difference. This role is antithetical to that of melodrama, in which the audience is supposed to be morally galvanized in defiance of a lucid threat. Though the villains of the new melodrama of globalization may not look like the twisty-mustachioed figures of the nineteenth-century melodrams with helpful names like Moneygrub or Bloodgood, they may nonetheless be unsubtle visions of greed and exploitation that are morally separate from the audience. In my earlier chapter, the "evil out there" was a neoliberal urban development bearing down on the Kims' convenience store; in this chapter the evil is realized in *Sheep*'s broad parody of merciless capitalism, which is supposed to be rejected by the presumably ethically conscious capitalism of the audience (who of course wouldn't *consider* buying fish-sticks from "Oceans Unlimited," the greedy corporation that owns the ship in the play). This assumed affiliation permits the audience to imagine themselves outside of *that* globalization, as morally superior to a captain and the crew who are morally bankrupt and baldly racist enough to have been lifted from a nineteenth-century melodrama. The melodramatic poetics have placed the audience on Razack's "high moral ground."

When MacKenzie was asked by critic Richard Ouzounian for his thoughts about *KONY 2012*, he signalled a desire to avoid the video's focus on the white knight: "It's pretty self-involved," he noted, "but that's the story of my generation, isn't it? 'Look how much I'm into this!' I would hope we can speak to people in a more meaningful way."[67] His play achieves this by offering a complex portrait of Saa as a distant stranger, not as a melodramatic villain or a suffering victim, but as someone trying to do right despite his unfortunate circumstances. The scenes of Saa tutoring his young sister Sia, are, on the other hand, melodramatic in the historical sense, in that they repeat the trope of pure "spaces of innocence" that must be protected against the evil world (much like the scenes in *KONY 2012* with Russell's cherubic son Gavin).[68] A further challenge to the audience's achieving a more meaningful ethical engagement in the play is the peculiar fact of Nick being an unlikable, hedonistic chauvinist, even at the dramatic cost of this being an unlikely fit with his otherwise do-gooder personality. This paradox allows the possibility that it isn't Nick's naîveté that undoes the humanitarian quest but simply his weak character. Whatever the intention of MacKenzie's choice, it has the effect of shielding the audience from the suggestion that its own desires may be at issue, that its own well-meaning interest may be misplaced, that its own complacency may, somehow, have implications for these distant strangers.

That the journey narrative is so bleakly represented draws a pessimistic portrait of the possibilities of global ethics. Early in the play, Nick suggests that he hates volunteering, because "the only thing people wanted from me was money … I wasn't helping anybody."[69] Subtly but noticeably, Nick is not interrogated for his false colonialist assumptions or poor knowledge of his context but for his underestimation of the world's villainy. Salverson has worried about this as well, wondering if trauma is somehow always located in a more real and threatening "out there," a place always away from the audience. Another distant stranger in the play is the more purely evil villain, the Butcher of Liberia, whose absence contributes to the sense of there being a nebulous, undefinable evil "out there" at the edge of the dramatic world, at the limits of the audience's awareness. The suggestion that trauma is "out there" seems also to be the sub-textual implication of Nick's question to Saa – "Saa, how did it feel to kill someone?"[70] – as though he needed to go to Africa to learn about murder; and also the implication of other pronouncements about Africa's difference, such as "even asthma is different in Africa,"[71] and "the girls don't dance like that in Toronto."[72]

The play's most self-aware moment comes when Saa accuses Nick of coming to Africa "bursting with sympathy" only to leave "invigorated"[73] – a challenge the audience might have understood to be issued at them as well. Failing to register that challenge, however, Christopher Hoile wrote in response to the Cahoots production of the play in the *Globe and Mail*: "What *SIA* and MacKenzie's own personal experience show is that the very comfort Westerners live in prevents us from understanding the depths of horror people in other countries experience every day."[74] Horror, as Salverson had worried, is "out there" while "we" live in comfort. If Hoile's response is representative of that of others, it is possible that the "script" of Western humanitarianism, and the historically rooted trope of the white knight, simply overwhelmed a challenge in the play that was too muted to meaningfully trouble its audience. Like Salverson, Razack experienced this ethical conundrum herself when she went to see an art exhibit about the Rwandan genocide. She found herself in the uncomfortable position of being called upon by the exhibit to perform her care as a compassionate witnesses to trauma. "From our position as witness," she wrote, reflecting on the experience, "we help to mark out the terrain of what is good and what is evil. Possessed of unique sensibilities, sensibilities that take us to the depths of grief and trauma, we can diagnose the trouble and act as the advance scout and the go-between."[75]

The new melodrama of globalization, it might be suggested, whatever its ethical shortcomings, still serves a pedagogical function; we do get to know something about some particular distant strangers. Salverson is of the opinion, however, that although "important material evidence may be presented … a generative engagement between performer and audience is unlikely."[76] Even without our accepting such a bleak prognosis, these plays seem to mourn the loss of unimpeachable virtue. This mourning has been observed of both contemporary and historical forms of melodrama: Christof Decker, for instance, explains that cinematic melodrama today is a backward-looking, nostalgic genre that emphasizes a sense of loss and creates pity for characters who, through forces such as modernization and urbanization, have become victims or outsiders.[77] And there may be something comparably mournful about the journey narrative as well; Mary Louise Pratt notes that the narrative descendants of nineteenth-century travel literature in contemporary culture tend toward a "bitter nostalgia for lost idioms of discovery."[78] A sense of failure looms large over the journey narrative, and the failure is at least a means of staging a *thematic* ethics: in *SIA*, the failure of Nick's mission to Ghana, his confrontation with an intractable situation, and his coming to awareness of his own naïveté give the play a means of interrogating its own staging of distant strangers. Without judging *SIA* or any other single example of the new melodrama of globalization too harshly, however, should we be concerned that so many plays feature failed journeys and failures of ethics? Especially when the emphasis repeatedly falls on the suffering not of distant strangers but of white knights, and by extension, on the audience's own traumatic witnessing?

If Canadian theatre develops a canon of white knight stories in which the staging of distant strangers allows audiences only to perform their outrage at a dystopian globalization, to pity helpless victims in endangered "spaces of innocence," or to revile cold-blooded deckhands and barbaric warlords, then it will fall short of making the powerful contribution it might otherwise make to the critical ethical issues of our time. Arendt felt that soliciting "pity" (rather than her more actionable "compassion") could have only two equally undesirable outcomes: that "spectators" do nothing, or that they develop, to use Boltanski's description of Arendt, "a benevolent concern for the unfortunate, without this being describable as a politics."[79]

A theatre of global ethics is capable of arousing more than benevolent concern. At performances of the plays I have discussed here I have sometimes heard audience members emit an audible sound in response to objectionable representations – a vocalization issued from a "moral high ground." But a performed moral sophistication is not an ethics. In at least a comparable manner to how multiculturalism generated a public fantasy of cosmopolitanism – one that had been emptied of the possibility of conflict or negotiation – the new melodrama enables a fantasy, to borrow Hans-Thies Lehmann's phrase, "of being able to preside quite calmly over all realities."[80]

CONCLUSION: MORAL COSMOPOLITANISM

A nineteenth-century performance tradition that competed with classical stage melodramas for audiences was the so-called Human Zoo, the ethnographic exhibitions of "tribal" people typically presented at world fairs in pre-modern "spaces of innocence" – the happy subjects of Empire. The anthropologist Ray Corbey, theorizing the kind of cultural "looking" that these performances invited, describes what he calls an "optical empiricism," which affirmed the colonial authority of viewers by configuring them as disinterested and omniscient panopticons.[81] As one motto of the 1893 Chicago World's Fair had it, "to see is to know." A century on, an ethically conscious theatre that has abandoned such overtly racist practices may still perpetuate the notion that the visibility of the distant stranger easily translates into knowledge and compassion. Through the emotive force of such features as strong emotionalism and extravagant expression, attention to a subject is imagined to produce some change in relationship or some corrected pattern of action. To modify the World's Fair motto for the new melodrama of globalization, we might propose "to see is to care," or, as Russell said in justification of *KONY 2012*, "in order for the people to care, they have to know, and they will only know if Kony's name is everywhere."[82] I have meant this chapter to give pause to allow us to consider how theatre is engaging with global ethics. Like Megan Boler who, with her critique of how empathy is "taught" in educational contexts, rejects Martha Nussbaum's idea that we can "know the other" simply through "compassion," I too have "significantly less faith in our capacity to judge what is 'really happening' to others."[83]

This is not to undermine the virtue of using theatre to build ethical relationships with distant strangers. Nor is it a rejection of poetic realism as an approach to doing so. On the contrary, it is to think about how this might be done in ways that avoid the hazards of departicularization or dehistoricization, of making the witness the important victim, or of positioning the audience as morally detached or even superior. In *Land of Strangers*, Ash Amin argues that the fact that a "politics of care" for the distant stranger might sometimes fall short of its aspirations, that this should not "exonerate the self-regarding, indifferent and incurious society"; on the contrary, given "stubborn impediments" to its working, "we need to turn to different processes and spaces of affiliation."[84] It is possible to put theatre to the service of global ethics while keeping watch for the many shoals on which it may be shipwrecked.

Jacqueline Lo and Helen Gilbert, who use the term "moral cosmopolitanism" more or less in the same way that I use "global ethics," speak about a tension between "the promise of cosmopolitanism as the enactment of universal communitas and its limits as a theory of embodied material praxis," by which they mean that staging strangers necessarily introduces irresolvable ethical complexities.[85] This is a problem, in fact, that many have raised in objection to the French philosopher Emmanuel Levinas's ethics (and which I addressed briefly in chapter 1). Levinas had reformulated Western ethics from a concern with the self to a concern with the other. On the surface, this reformulation would avoid Eagleton's "customary Western vice" of self-interest and shift the emphasis toward fulfilling one's obligation to the other. Levinas, though, had proposed that this obligation was infinite, extending to anyone and everyone – a beautiful formulation that is difficult in practice and can only reconcile itself to failure. As others have pointed out before me, theatre is perhaps one place where we can try to meet the infinite responsibility in human, indeed personal terms, portraying empathy for everyone through empathy for specific people in specific places.[86] Theatre is a container for staging the absurd failure to meet the necessary but impossible call of Levinas's infinite responsibility, but there may be ways, as Samuel Beckett famously put it, to "fail again, fail better."[87]

In a Canadian theatre in which plays that feature dark threats, white knights, and distant strangers are appearing with frequency, there is reason to think carefully about the relationship with strangers that its theatrical strategies propose to audiences. I have tried to illustrate some ways in which these strategies implicate their audiences as a means of thinking through theatre's engagement with global ethics. In keeping with my characterization of the new melodrama of globalization, Lo and Gilbert note that moral cosmopolitanism in performance has focused more on "feeling" or "thinking" globally, and has engaged less with the "embodied realities of people groups, cultures and practices."[88] The problem has to do with a tension that runs throughout this book between the particular and the general, between strangers' placement in a material context and their becoming a generalized arch-metaphor of difference. Rather than being a problem, this may be a resource in that theatre forms a bridge between the local, in the sense of the local community and the immediacy of a performance context; and the global, in the sense of a larger political community and also the symbolic. But to recall an issue raised in chapter 1, theatre needs to be mindful of the kind of universalism to which its representations appeal. Lo and Gilbert's "feeling" and "thinking" globally is a subtle allusion to the need for a refocus, in the manner of Levinas, away from the self. In a like spirit, I have tried to show how white knights turn toward the self and thereby stage distant strangers as tragic and dehistoricized victims in need of rescue.

Whatever the challenges, the prevalence of plays staging morally conflicted journeys elsewhere in the world demonstrates a need for a robust global ethics. In *The Globalization of Strangeness*, Chris Rumford says artists are themselves the new "cosmopolitan strangers" able to "connect people with distant others [and] betoken new forms of social solidarity, and who can maneuver in the restricted spaces caused by the social and political compression characteristic of the Global Age."[89] Indeed, what the new melodrama of globalization itself bears witness to is that, in a time of keen disenfranchisement with politics, the ethical has taken up home in art with renewed vigour. The responsibility of the artist here is not only to be asking these questions but also to let the answers lead to new forms, new narratives, new aesthetics. In the coming chapter, I consider possibilities for staging strangers in a surprising and fresh fashion that, for artists and audience alike, can be a difficult and indeterminate encounter with difference.

5

Making Strange: The "Active" Audience

Drifted subjectivity is a vision of the world that breaks down the oppositions between spectator and actor, self and other, here and there. It does not seek to colonize … but instead recognizes the mutuality of responsibility and seeks to overcome the sovereignty of the self. The drifted self – the drifted spectator – retains agency (not simply the appearance of agency) and yet understands that she is un-apart from the pains of others, even if these are not fully comprehended, and indeed that she is constituted in relation to this pain.

Emma Willis, "Emancipated Spectatorship and Subjective Drift"[1]

SMALL GESTURES WITH BIG MEANING

After watching a performance of Jovanni Sy's site-specific play *A Taste of Empire*, members of the audience, including myself, were asked to make a choice.[2] We had gathered at a demonstration kitchen in Toronto's St Lawrence Market and had just watched Sy, in character as sous-chef "Jovanni," cook a traditional Filipino dish called *rellenong bangus* live in front of us. The dish, a milkfish stuffed with ingredients foreign to the Philippines, had become a metaphor for American colonization in the country, and a metaphor also for the general corporatization of food at the expense of labourers such as Jovanni, the sous-chef himself. As chef Jovanni prepped the ingredients, he related the history of the ingredients and the story of the various labourers implicated in their production. Among them were Carlos, the Mexican migrant apple-farm worker (who was briefly personalized by having his image projected on a screen overhead and having some of his life story shared with the audience) and Piag the Filipino fisherman (who had to abandon his hand-line fishing practice to work in an industrial processing plant). Sympathizing with these strangers as he went, chef Jovanni had an increasingly difficult time shilling for the sleazy corporation for which he worked, Imperial Seafood, and he began to rebel. With the dish fully prepared at the end of the show, Jovanni invited the audience up to taste the *rellenong bangus*, a gesture that the performance had coded with ethical implications. On the one hand, the audience could choose to share in a momentary community with the performers and fellow members of the audience by tasting the dish; on the other, the performance had presented the dish as a product of both colonial history and the exploitative labour of strangers, in which, by tasting, the audience would implicated. Like most other spectators who had attended the performance that night, I chose to eat.

Such small gestures of participation laden with big meaning are one means through which contemporary theatre is experimenting with the ethical relationship between the stage and audience. This trend carries forward a tradition of experiment in twentieth-century Western theatre that saw a series of influential practitioners imagine aesthetics and practices that would create a more "active" audience. Brecht's Epic Theatre, for instance, was a corrective for what Brecht saw as a "bourgeois theatre" that lulled its audiences to sleep with theatrical poetic realism and force-fed them conservative values.[3] Augusto Boal, as another example, imagined how spectators could become "spect-actors" who could literally come onstage to interrupt the representation and play out different possibilities themselves.[4] But the more recent vogue for what are variously called immersive, participatory, relational or site-specific performance practices represents a new wave of experimentation with activating the audience.

Claims that an active audience is an ethically engaged audience, such as James Thompson's suggestion in his *Performance Affects* that the intimacy of participatory forms creates their ethical force,[5] tend to come packaged within larger sociological arguments about the need for performance to contribute to a reinvigorated public sphere. In something of the same way that Doreen Massey has observed a romanticization of the local in response to a threatening globalization, the active audience is aligned with a set of warm and attractive social values. Describing that gesture, Matthew Reason writes that, "the 'goodness' of the participatory audience in this context can mean variously politically good (empowered), ethically good (empathetic), creatively good (not reactionary), perhaps even good in terms of wellbeing (physically active)."[6] Correspondingly, there is a way in which an "active" audience may imagine itself occupying a "moral high ground" of a different order, one based on a willingness to co-create with artists in a shared, public encounter.

However, as I suggested in my account of *The Stranger* in the Prologue, the ethical potential of even the most intensely participatory practices is far from guaranteed. In this chapter I take a more cleareyed look at how participatory practices – broadly imagined – produce their audience's presence and agency in encounters with strangers.[7] Participatory practices, which have long been the norm in the world of performance art, have in recent years become common in mainstream theatre as well. This increased engagement has occasioned a number of new critiques of how the audience is activated in these practices – how it is asked to move, to watch, to contribute – all of which have implications for the ethics of encounter with difference. In an influential essay published in *Artforum* in 2007, the French philosopher Jacques Rancière argued that even supposedly passive spectators sitting in the dark can be "emancipated" because they do active, interpretive work in imagining themselves into the world of the play.[8] Indeed, it is odd to think that, simply by standing and moving, a spectator would automatically have a heightened ethical relationship to a representation. The fact that small gestures of the sort at the end of *A Taste of Empire* can be so coded with meaning is in itself perhaps a symptom of the over-dominance of the practice of sitting in a darkened auditorium (itself a product of fairly recent theatre history). In that performance, the eating of the *rellenong bangus* lent an experiential metaphor to the participant-spectator's implication in colonialism and other invisible global networks of production. There nevertheless remains plenty of reason to be skeptical about *A Taste of Empire*'s invitation to eat and other like gestures that call on our involvement. Jen Harvie, for one, has argued that large-scale immersive theatre productions (such as those produced by the UK's explosively popular Punchdrunk Theatricals) are, in effect, offloading the labour of the performance onto the audience, which is complicit in rather than critical of a wider system of the neoliberal exploitation of precarious labour.[9] Building on Harvie's critique, Keren Zaiontz has argued convincingly that such productions do not offer the audience meaningful ethical choices, but calculate the spectator as a professional consumer, or "prosumer," because "the choices (and subsequent responses) are oriented around how best to consume the production."[10] It may not be so easy for performance to create meaningful public ethical encounter without a reflexive appeal to over-romanticized compensatory ideas about intimacy, the local, community, or democracy.

What Harvie and Zaiontz don't particularly address, and what I take up in this chapter, is the positive potential that we can imagine in participatory theatre practices for staging strangers. I look here at two examples, completely different in nature and subject matter, each of which presents a unique strategy for escaping at least those problems that arise within the melodramatic poetics described in the previous chapter: *Nightmare/Dream*, a site-specific performance by Toronto's It's a Freedom Thing Theatre (hereafter, IFT Theatre), and *The Global Savages*, a project of the Debajehmujig Storytellers based on Manitoulin Island in Ontario. These both push beyond the popular poetic realism of Canadian theatre and steer clear of an "aesthetic of injury" that presents the stranger as victim and the audience as compassionate witnesses, as in the plays discussed earlier. A look at these examples helps historicize Canadian theatre's current obsession with ethics, in particular global ethics. How do these performances produce and codify the stranger's presence and actions, and in turn, "our" own? Do their different ways of calling upon our bodies produce only an illusory seeing, knowing, or caring?

THE KALEIDOSCOPY OF A DRIFTED SUBJECTIVITY

In the Epilogue to his book *Postdramatic Theatre*, Hans-Thies Lehmann offers his thoughts on the possibility of an ethical and political (he says "ethico-political") "postdramatic theatre," a theatre distinguished by its reliance on elements of performance other than narrative tensions of dramatic conflict for its effect. Lehmann suggests that in postdramatic theatre, the ethico-political is to be found neither in thematizing global issues nor in polemic or activist argument. These, he writes, "belong in the domain of real politics not represented politics."[11] Nor does the ethico-political reside in intercultural theatre, which he unfortunately too narrowly conceives as a European tradition of avant-garde intercultural artists such as Peter Brook and Arianne Mnouchkine. For Lehmann, the path to the ethico-political is in theatre's troubling of the "mode of representation" itself. Although he begins the chapter by saying he will avoid sociological readings of the present moment, he proceeds (in a line of thought agreeing with Bauman) to suggest that in a deeply mediatized twenty-first century, theatre has a new duty to interrupt passive spectatorship and consumption of narratives by exposing the mechanisms of our watching and perception; "the politics of theatre is a politics of perception," he writes.[12] Lehmann sees traditional "dramatic" theatre as an inadequate representation of contemporary political realities. In its place, he suggests, a properly political aesthetic needs to interrupt social and political order, to transgress the rules and introduce chaos. The dramatic tradition verbalizes and rationalizes contemporary realities, whereas the role of theatre should be to exploit complexity and chaos, to "'dramatize' the uncertainty."[13] Lehmann observes a relationship between poetics and epistemic political and sociological conditions, and, for him, any satisfactions that tragedy and drama may have offered in a previous time and place no longer satisfy. Postdramatic theatre need not involve any gestures of participation, but neither does it exclude them. Lehmann proposes a "politics of perception," an ethically active mode of engaging spectators whose attention is turned toward theatre's own mechanisms of signification, and how these realize social or moral values.[14] Lehmann's call here is for an ethical spectatorship – what I called a "responsible looking" in the previous chapter. Lehmann's ethical spectatorship would permit a direct relationship between refreshed perceptions of an indeterminate representation and refreshed perceptions of the world it reflects. His argument has problems on both sides, however. It underestimates the ways in which "dramatic theatre" may be subtly ethico-political; for instance, the way melodrama may usefully make a complex world morally legible and actionable for an audience; and it also overestimates the ethical potential of postdramatic forms of performance, a misjudgment that in some cases may alienate audiences to the point of working against their active engagement, or, in Lehmann's useful coinage, their "response-ability."[15] It needs to be appreciated that, at least for some members of an audience, there will be an upper limit to the extent of difficulty and indeterminacy they will accept. Still, the sociological context in which Lehmann situates his argument resonates with the context of globalization I have evoked throughout this book.

The ethical potential of Lehmann's politics of perception seemed to be just what was at stake in IFT Theatre's *Nightmare/Dream*, a site-specific performance staged in Toronto's Campbell House first in January 2013, and in a second and slightly modified version in the same venue in January 2014. Although it did not frame itself in Lehmann's terms, *Nightmare/Dream* was postdramatic for not relying on story or dramatic tension, and for immersing the audience in highly physically choreographed scenes sequenced seemingly only by a tonal or emotional logic. *Nightmare/Dream* features the story of a young African immigrant, Simon Dube, who, after receiving news of his father's death in Africa, embarks on a psychic journey back to Africa in nightmare/dream–like fashion, moving between contemporary and historical visions of himself. The visions do not come together in any explicit narrative and move freely between these different contexts, their only common element being the "dreaming" character of Simon, whom the audience – numbering only about twenty-five people for each performance – accompanies on the journey. While some portions of it were playful, the piece was for the most part meditative and hypnotic in keeping with the conceit of the dream. It was developed visually through a "storyboarding" process, but the text also underscored the atmosphere with a clipped, poetic-style written by Toronto-based multimedia artist Motion.

Elements of the piece connect it both to the generational family drama and to the new melodramas of globalization. Like the second-generation protagonists of *Mother Tongue*, *Singkil*, and *Kim's Convenience* in chapter 2, Simon is torn between his ancestral past (we only know he is from Africa) and different versions of the present, in which he must perform demanding social and professional identities. Just as in *The Sheep and the Whale*, the Africa of *Nightmare/Dream* is a place of ritual, tradition, and pre-modernity, such that by clinging to it, Simon is clinging also to a stable subjectivity. In a clear reiteration of Hassan's vision of the Aid ritual of sacrifice in *Sheep*, in which Hassan's cultural authenticity and loyalty is tested when he is handed a knife to cut a calf's throat, Simon in *Nightmare/Dream* appears at his late father's funeral in Africa and is handed a knife by a tribal dancer and urged to sacrifice a calf. Unable to play his role, Simon symbolically severs his connection to home, and sets out on a journey through time and space to locate himself.

What is different about *Sheep* and *Nightmare/Dream*, however, are the aesthetics of the representations and the way the audience is positioned in relation to them. While Ghazali's *Sheep*, in keeping with other examples of the new melodrama of globalization, constructed a "morally legible" dramatic universe that places strangers "out there" and casts the audience as compassionate witnesses, *Nightmare/Dream* effects a less stable encounter. In fact, *Nightmare/Dream* is an aesthetic – and, by extension, also an ethical – deconstruction of its more melodramatic cousin. It upsets the popular convention of the travelling and virtuously suffering white knight character by instead making the traveller the stranger whose journey takes the audience through the layers of colonial history. As a result, the audience's position in relation to the representation is indeterminate and uncertain. As much as Simon appears divided between an ancestral African heritage and a present Canadian life, these are not positions between which he must choose but sedimented historical and psychic layers of identity that attach to the present. As the stranger figure, Simon does not become a victim of modernity to be rescued. As he meanders through myth and history he takes up a place at various thresholds: he is hailed as an "other" when, as a PhD student teaching a university course on African history, he is addressed by his students as a foreigner (they ask where he is *really* from); he becomes a nineteenth-century black middleman merchant collaborating with a white slave owner; he waltzes with and seduces a 1960s-era youthful Queen Elizabeth; and becomes the confident leader of an unnamed and recently liberated African nation. As in the generational family drama, the play is a story of Simon's reckoning with the death of a parent and the associated disconnection from culture and history. However, *Nightmare/Dream* avoids what Lehmann derides as an "immediate morality." It offers no clear solutions to Simon's disconnection; nor, in the play's larger geopolitical imaginary, does it present any easy resolution between Africa and the West or between a colonial history and the present.[16]

5.1 Peter Bailey as Simon Dube (centre) delivering a speech as the leader of a liberated African nation, with the Dancer (Pulga Muchochoma) and the Singer (Neema Bickersteth) in It's a Freedom Thing Theatre's *Nightmare/Dream*.

As a result, Simon's plural positioning throughout history makes complex the audience's own relationship to his shifting dramatic world. The audience's kaleidoscopic perspective on Simon's lives, past and present, permits a productive ambivalence of a sort that Helena Grehan has argued allows for a "radical unsettlement, an experience of disruption and interruption in which the anodyne is challenged."[17] Emma Willis has theorized a similar idea in her work on the ethics of bearing witness to traumatic representations, finding in the work of American playwright Erik Ehn what she calls a "drifted subjectivity," in which an "I" and a "you" are deliberately confused by the representation.[18] Such drifted subjectivity specifically disrupts any easy process by which, in Willis's words quoted in the epigraph to this chapter, "the subject of witness becomes the virtue of the witness," thereby breaking down "oppositions between spectator and actor, self and other, here and there."[19] The result is an active looking at looking – Lehmann's "politics of perception" – a spectatorship that asks the audience to adopt a contingent, changing perspective.

Nightmare/Dream offers more than a drifted subjectivity that shifts from one clearly identifiable position to another; it provides a kaleidoscopic subjectivity of mutually compatible realities. This was tangibly realized in the piece's third scene, in which Simon assumes the role of a nineteenth-century black trader who collaborates with a white slave owner. The scene took place in the Campbell House dining room, a rectangular room with a brick hearth and a long table that had a bountiful spread for the scene, the centrepiece of which was the calf's head from the funeral ritual for Simon's father. Lured into the dining room by the voice of a singer singing "Amazing Grace" (who transforms into a house servant who we learn is actually the landowner's house slave), Simon accepts the landowner's invitation to sit at the table as the audience follow him in and distribute themselves around the room. The two performers enjoy the colonial bounty – rum, tea, sugar – and discuss in a poetic repartee the business of the slave trade and the quelling of colonial insurrection. The singer-as-slave interjects in the dialogue to name what isn't being said – that she herself is like the chattel they are discussing, having been sold and bartered like cocoa or diamonds – and she goes unacknowledged by the others in the scene. Meanwhile, adding to the visual and auditory kaleidoscopy of the scene, the tribal dancer from the previous scene who had performed at the funeral of Simon's father is crouched beneath the table, seemingly with no freedom to move, meekly, silently cowering in either anger or pain. The "house slave's" resumed rendition of "Amazing Grace" and the dancer's moans exert a pull on Simon that sees him suddenly revolt against the slave trader for having stolen his freedom. Becoming aware of how he, in the character of the black trader, has become complicit in his own oppression, Simon triumphantly declares at the end of the scene, citing Jomo Kenyatta, the first African president of Kenya: "When the Missionaries arrived, the Africans had the land and the Missionaries had the Bible. They taught how to pray with our eyes closed. When we opened them, they had the land and we had the Bible."

Offering this kaleidoscopic perspective on Simon would be just as possible in a "traditional" theatrical configuration in which the audience doesn't move, and indeed, much about *Nightmare/Dream* seemed as if it would have been possible on a traditional stage. But the audience's physical positioning around the scenes of the piece at some points further heightened a consciousness of overlapping frames of reference. In the scene described above, any of the participants might have been standing behind Simon, the white slave owner, and would have had to reposition themselves to be able to see the tribal dancer under the table. This mutability of perspective, and the need to take on different points of view, was felt throughout the performance. In the first scene, the audience seemed to be cast as students in Simon's history class; in the next they were attendees at his father's African funeral and witnesses to an ancient ritual; then they were eavesdropping on a colonial conversation, and later they became the jubilant citizens of a recently liberated African nation. *Nightmare/Dream* was more immersive than participatory, and if we ask, as Gareth White has, what exactly are we "immersed in" in immersive theatre, the answer could be the psychic experience of the stranger "at the threshold,"[20] or perhaps the psychic experience of Rumford's "strangeness," the sociological condition in which the "here" and "there," "us" and "them," have become less certain.

I hesitate, however, to claim ethical significance for *Nightmare/Dream*'s immersive strategies. There was a seductive quality to the performance, the proximity of strangers in the audience charging the experience with a novel excitement, the hyper-presence of a shared journey into an unknown experience. Of course the venue did, in this case, have rich significance: attending the performance in a colonial mansion that sits in the shadow of mirrored office buildings aroused a consciousness that the power structures that were materialized in the play's historical visions remain part of the deep structure of the city's architecture and geography. A hypnotizing soundscape also contributed a meditative quality. In *Nightmare/Dream* the stranger takes on an uncanny presence whose liminality and tenuous hold on the spectator's consciousness is physical, visceral, and sensory. This tenuousness is what differentiates *Nightmare/Dream* from other representations of strangers described in this book, where the terms of the strangers' inclusion or exclusion are made more explicit and legible. The nonprofessional culturally focused theatres, for instance, are clearly themselves positioned "outside" the dominant culture, and the self-realizations of some of the generational family dramas clearly stake a claim on the public "recognition" of a coherent cultural identity. But does – or should – the hyper-presence and felt intimacy of *Nightmare/Dream* constitute any claim on knowing or caring for strangers? The alternative that *Nightmare/Dream* offers to the new melodrama of globalization is a diffused subjectivity, a politics of perception that refuses familiar modes of looking and any attendant notions of knowing or caring. Of course a danger here is that the performance's reflexivity may have estranged the audience and therefore lost its opportunity for social significance. The question becomes: how can performance avoid commoditizing or fetishizing intimacy in encounters with strangers?

At least in the Canadian context, where calls to global ethics (at least in mainstream theatre) can slip into a melodramatic poetics, *Nightmare/Dream*'s disavowal of any easy knowing or caring seems to be precisely its important contribution. An outcome of ethico-political theatre, Lehmann offers, is that theatre may confront binaries of here and there, inside and outside (just as with Willis's "drifted subjectivity"), with a "move toward the *mutual implication of actors and spectators in the theatrical production of images.*" Such an experience, he writes, "would be not only aesthetic but therein at the same time ethico-political."[21] Certainly *Nightmare/Dream* was careful about how it called upon the audience to look (as it made many positions available) and it was judicious also about its invitations to participate. While the audience's being gently led through the performance spaces by performers made it participatory in a basic sense, the audience was not called upon to interact with the performers or make a gesture like the decision to taste in *A Taste of Empire* described at the start of the chapter; that is, a gesture coded to take on a particular meaning in relation to the stranger. In *Nightmare/Dream* the audience had to learn the performance's "cues" as it went, tacitly and silently moving more or less together, all of which lent an edge of collective uncertainty. One simple gesture of participation came during a scene in the basement of the colonial house, which took place around a large wooden table next to a roaring hearth. The audience entered the room with Simon, to find the singer from the earlier scenes pouring cups of tea that Simon handed out to members of the audience to drink. A window leading outside was open, letting modern traffic sounds bleed into the historical scene – and also the cold January air, which made steam rise from the cups. In the dialogue that ends the piece, the singer and Simon have an exchange remarkably similar to the exchange between the Doctor and the Stowaway from *The Sheep and the Whale* cited in the previous chapter:

> SINGER: What is your name?
> SIMON: La-hoa white man.
> SINGER: No that is not your name.
> SIMON: Chattel.
> SINGER: No that is not your name.
> SIMON: Slaver.
> SINGER: No that is not your name.
> SIMON: Trader.
> SINGER: No that is not your name.
> SIMON: Saviour.
> SINGER: No that is not your name.
> *He whispers in her ear. She slowly smiles. Simon sits at the bench by the table. Singer gets a pail of water and washes Simon's face. She puts a pinch of sugar in his mouth and then some salt. She hands him a cup of tea. There is libation. Simon drinks and invites the audience to drink with him.*[22]

Like the Stowaway in *Sheep*, Simon at this moment is metaphysically located in a symbolic imaginary outside of history; but unlike the Stowaway, in the final whispered secret to the singer, and in his apparent moment of contentment shared with the audience, Simon seems to find some kind of momentary consolation. Staged differently, the moment could have read something like the over-coded moralistic self-realization of the kind found in *Singkil* (see chapter 2), in which the protagonist's navigation of multiple loyalties ends in a complete and performative self-possession. In *Nightmare/Dream* the moment resists collapsing into that conclusion by insisting on its kaleidoscopy – the mixing of modern sounds from outside with the historical scene within the house, the comfort of the colonial tea-ritual contrasting with the cold winter air, and the fact of Simon whispering an evidently satisfying answer exclusively to the singer. All these elements generate not the spurious intimacy of simple proximity or the clarity of straightforwardly coded gestures of interaction, but the precious and fleeting feeling of a shared, briefly settled moment of peace with a character who, in this final dignified moment, remains thickly entangled in his past and present conditions. What is powerful about *Nightmare/Dream* is that it offers a kind of looking that neither fully claims – nor fully abdicates – seeing or knowing strangers. It offers what Matthew Reason calls a "detached opticality" that is active, that does not, as proponents of participatory theatre practices might sometimes have it, turn spectators into "passive and disengaged spectators."[23] The audience occupies no singular position, no "high moral ground" from which to observe Simon as a victim, and there is no single "lesson" to glean about Western colonialism or the humanitarian journey. Simon does not float through history to become an object of white guilt or a talisman of the audience's enacted shame. Rather than being completely de-particularized and removed from history, his subjectivity slides through history, while remaining rooted in specific and symbolically resonant sites.

In the process, "we" as an audience do not harden into any one attitude or perspective, and no assumptions are thrust upon us about Simon's relationship to history. As Willis has put it, the performance has left us "nicely confused" about where we stand as individual spectators. By refusing the audience any stable "we," the performance has not tried, as some forms of immersive or participatory performance do, to generate temporary fellow feeling or momentary relationships among spectators. Beyond the simple pleasure of having shared in an affecting and ambiguous experience together for a short time, spectators' presence has not been produced in any prescribed or familiar fashion. In terms of the way gestures of participation may generate a more "active" ethics, *Nightmare/Dream* differs sharply, however, from my next example.

MAKING STRANGE IN *THE GLOBAL SAVAGES*

To situate aesthetic choices within a sociological context (as Lehmann wrote that he wouldn't but did anyway), my interest in Simon's drifted subjectivity connects back to the discussion in chapter 1 about the plural nature of identity in a globalized world. In *The Land of Strangers*, Ash Amin argues that, while contemporary "belonging" is more plural than in the past, it is no less strong or passionately felt than a more nationality- or ethnicity-based affiliation. "Any venture into new alliances and allegiances," he writes, "requires an affective link, one that can be nourished by openness to fruitful exchange with the unknown and distant. And this occurs especially when there is a common interest or concern, binding strangers emotionally even if not personally."[24] Amin looks at new ways in which we can relate to and detach from space strategically, and how we adopt new styles of affiliation among strangers to maintain overlapping local and global loyalties. His sense of "relational" identification sings in unison with Doreen Massey's "ethics of place" (also discussed in chapter 1), which similarly promotes a "relational geography" that can be aware of the globalism and rootedness of place at once.[25] The key to activities in this spirit, Massey suggests, is to avoid the twin pitfalls of local romanticism and rootless cosmopolitan globalism. We should bear in mind, too, the ethical implication of a performance that gives us license to imagine how we may "calmly preside over all realities,"[26] when not all identities, roles, or realities are visible or available to anyone. A kaleidoscopic vision that enables us to relate in multiple ways, to see through multiple lenses, she implies, is preferable to one that would anticipate a particular moral attitude.

An example that configures its audience's participation, presence, and intimacy completely differently – and yet in a related way – is Debajehmujig Storytellers' *The Global Savages.* The Debajehmujig Storytellers (hereafter, Debaj) are an Anishinaabe theatre collective on the Wikwemikong Unceded Indian Reserve on Manitoulin Island who maintain a practice that is both deeply local and global in orientation.[27] Their *Global Savages* project was created in part to make their style of performative storytelling responsive to the places to which they travel. It was also a response to the way indigenous peoples have been made strange within mainstream Canadian culture. In keeping with Alan Filewod's "maturation story" of Canadian culture mentioned at the start of chapter 2, Debaj was aware that indigenous art didn't seem to "count" until it had historically been "recognized" (as if there had been no indigenous performance before playwrights such as Tomson Highway wrote plays adopting a Western dramaturgy). To interrupt that story, Debaj wanted their new project to tell instead the "18,000 Year Animated Oral History of the Indigenous

People of North America aka Turtle Island in 90 Minutes or Less." The performance they created is a storytelling encounter with an audience which features four characters of Anishinaabe legend (the "Global Savages" of the title): Debajehmud the Storyteller, Mudjeekwis the Record Keeper, Chibiabos the Musician, and Sky Woman the Mother. In the playful ninety-minute performance at the centre of the project, the four relate and explain some Anishinaabe legends, always making an effort to connect these stories to the context in which they find themselves. To date, the Global Savages have taken their story to Scotland, the Netherlands, France, and across Canada to locations from British Columbia to Nova Scotia.

In each location, the characters do more than just put on their performance; they take to the streets as well, appearing in public contexts in their traditional Anishinaabe clothing to learn what they can about the place they are in, and to seek out encounters with strangers in public. In these interactions they maintain their mythical "characters," although the line between character and the actors' own identities as Anishinaabek is not clearly drawn. And they do this *before* they perform because the idea of the project is that these interactions will inform and shape the way they tell their story in that place. The interactions are documented in image and video – by their producer and photographer Ron Berti – and watched by whoever happens to be around, so they take on a performative dimension in spite of their informality. Also, the group does a "sunrise walk," a ritual "entrance" to the place where they are staying, at dawn along a "significant route," and they welcome people from that place to join them. These interactions outside the formal performance create a meta-narrative of encounter around the project, such that Debaj's artists are encountered not just within the fictional frame of the performance but as travelling artists who are conduits and messengers of a culture and tradition. This works in two directions: to add a kind of extra significance to the more unmediated, unscripted social encounters of the project, as well as to make the performers more present as individuals within the performance proper. Any line delineating mythological characters from the actors' own lives, or any line between a symbolic order of representation and the "real" is consciously and deliberately blurred.

For this reason *The Global Savages* resists staging the stranger in the sense of staging a strictly theatrical encounter, and instead uses a set of performance practices as a multi-layered pretext for rich encounter between "fictional" and "real" strangers. They bring something quite different – something much more organic and indeterminate – than the rigidly coded gesture toward global ethics exhibited in the new melodramas of globalization. When I worked with Debaj on the Prague-Toronto-Manitoulin Theatre Project, I grew to understand that they construct their projects as they do on account of the critical importance of building relationships in all their encounters with audiences and fellow artists. In the world of professional arts, and certainly the world of expensive international exchanges in which time is often at a premium, given the expense of travel and accommodation, there is often a pressure to be expedient, to get to the work and the performance as efficiently as possible. Over the past decade, Debaj has made it a prerequisite for collaboration that unstructured, unpredictable time be spent getting to know one another. *The Global Savages* is thus designed to offer representation as a site of symbolic intercultural dialogue and also as a site of direct interpersonal exchange among strangers.

This is a fundamentally pedagogical design, not in the sense of a didactic approach, but in the sense that it unfolds the encounter socially and relationally, introducing, as Lehmann has suggested is necessary in a twenty-first-century context, an element of chaos. In stark contrast to the situations of the Multicultural Theatre Association's festivals, which offered up strangers speaking in foreign languages with no provision for understanding between them and their audience – *The Global Savages* consciously configures a "strangeness" that is not expected to "un-strange" itself during a brief performance. They are aware that their "audience" – though "audience" becomes an inadequate word to describe their relationship with those with whom they come in contact – is unfamiliar with them. In Europe in particular, audiences are typically familiar with indigenous North Americans only through the wildly distorted lens of Hollywood film, or through the stories of nineteenth-century German author Karel May, whose characters Winnetou and Old Shatterhand, popularized in a series of 1960s films, embodied the romanticized image of the stoic Indian and idealized a pre-industrial life threatened by European civilization.

If a romanticism about the local, or a folkloric framing of the local, would be problematic in staging the stranger, as I argued in chapter 2, then Debaj's choice to appear in their performances in traditional dress (which starkly sets them apart from the urban street settings in which they typically conduct their interventions) places them in danger of being regarded in the same fashion. Instead of having an antiquated image thrust upon them, however, they self-consciously wield that image to their advantage. Their decision to title the project *The Global Savages*, as opposed to *Global Aboriginals*, or *Natives*, or even the dated (although within their community, reclaimed) *Indians*, the dehumanizing older term by which they were hailed by their European colonizers, makes a deliberately anachronistic reference to the colonialism that necessarily haunts their encounters beyond their home community. It calls up Ahmed's "conditions that produce the stranger in the first place," a way of looking that necessarily looks back not in nostalgia but as a way of seeing the "now" being in dialogue with the "past." Despite their appearance, the artists respond to the present, interact with participants as individuals, and keep their traditions and stories alive in the moment of encounter. This strategy also permits a knitting together of the local and global in the sense that, wherever the Global Savages travel, they remain tethered to their own tradition and, as far as possible, to the place in which they find themselves. In a challenge to Massey's twin perils of the romantic local and the cosmopolitan global, *The Global Savages* playfully balances these simultaneously.

By choosing to appear in public in costume as the characters of Anishinaabe legend, the global savages cast themselves as strangers in a public drama. The way this calls upon their audiences to look at them and relate to them necessarily holds up a mirror to the society and culture with which they come into contact. The strategy is not unlike that used by Chicano performance artist Guillermo Gómez-Peña's La Pocha Nostra collective, which frequently deploys indigenous iconography in its performances as a way of performing a grotesque vision of the indigenous Other back to mainstream society. And there are some direct parallels between the work of the two groups. Gómez-Peña's most famous piece, *Undiscovered Amerindians*, his collaboration with Coco Fusco, had the two perform in a cage in museum settings pretending to "perform" the everyday activities of the Guantanari, a fictional tribe of indigenous people from a fictional island in the Gulf of Mexico. In 2003 Debaj's piece *Audge's Place* at the Art Gallery of Ontario recreated the actual living room of community elder and Debajehmujig community liaison Audrey Wemigwans in the gallery. In *Undiscovered Amerindians* and in many of their other performances, La Pocha Nostra describes this as a "reverse anthropology" – representations that cast the onlooker as the exoticized and exoticizing agent, as though the performance is enacting a fetishized fantasy of the stranger and sent up so far that its artificiality is exposed.[28] For both La Pocha Nostra and Debaj, drawing heavily on stereotype requires a delicate dance, particularly in performances creating only momentary encounters with spectators. "What prevents us," Gómez-Peña asks, "from becoming the very stylized freaks we are attempting to deconstruct or parody?"[29] Debaj runs the same risk in its visual presentation of the antiquated savage wherever in the world they use such imagery, but perhaps especially in Europe, where audiences have little direct knowledge of indigenous peoples. It becomes clear that, so as to avoid a collapse into uncritical romanticization, para-theatrical or pedagogical elements are necessary, elements that orbit the representations themselves in the form of dialogue, exchange, and informal time spent together to learn more about each other. The group's appearance as "savage" strangers deliberately amplifies their strangeness *in order to* occasion encounter.

But from here La Pocha Nostra and Debaj's strategies diverge. Where Pocha Nostra queers the "mainstream" with confrontational performances that defamiliarize whatever is "normal" in politics, culture, media, sexuality, and race relations, Debaj adopts a gentler aesthetic rooted in their culture's ancient practices of oral storytelling. In their view, the storyteller also wants to seize his or her audience's attention, but from there enters a casual relationship with the audience in which learning and sharing take place through informal exchange. This is an example, I think, of how ethical relationships can lead to the political in surprising ways. Gareth White, writing about immersive theatre, situates it within a strain of twentieth-century performance that sees "political potential inherent in the reordering of audience-performer relationships,"[30] and Lehmann, in his final chapter of *Postdramatic Theatre* dealing with ethics and politics, suggests that ethical potential lies specifically in introducing risk to performance along with a willingness to contravene social convention.[31] *The Global Savages*, though neither immersive nor postdramatic theatre, can be associated with these traditions in its pursuit of ethical encounter with audiences, but it is notable for its subtle approach to ethics. It does not offer a political provocation; nor does it ever call upon its audience to "empathize" with strangers as victims. This is a discomfort that works. They play the "savages" deftly; smoothly and almost unnoticeably, they slip between performing a stereotype, imparting a traditional teaching, and "dropping character" to interact socially with their audience.

The Global Savages demonstrates that the indeterminacy of ethics needn't come in the form of a confrontation or provocation, but can arise merely from an unusual encounter in unusual conditions and an openness to engage in a direct relationship with strangers. By so carefully wielding control over how they are being made strange, and using that control to more fully engage the spectator on a personal level, these strangers stage encounter on their own terms. The strategy of pulling the audience in with the surprising title and image of the "global savage" in order to more fully explain how their culture lives in relation to tradition, Debaj deftly knits together seeing, knowing, and caring for strangers without prescribing any particular attitudes or assuming any prior knowledge on the part of those they encounter.

CONCLUSION: ON "BEING THERE"

As I argued in my opening chapter, the globalization of Canadian theatre demands careful attention to the ethical dimensions of how theatre is staging difference. Especially in a "world city" such as Toronto, theatre has been serving as a critical forum for "making strange" the otherwise "normal" experience of difference in everyday life, the familiar "daily practice of mixing and rubbing elbows with difference," as Bauman has put it.[32] The symbolically charged spaces and practices of theatre have the advantage of making us aware of how encounters with difference make that difference, and make an "us" in relation to it. Theatre can enable different ways of understanding what or why difference *is*; the extent to which, for instance, it is a product of present and historical conditions and narratives. One of Amin's solutions to the frequency with which strangers are domesticated or rejected is to find, in what is a surprise turn toward representation in his otherwise sociological discussion, "new metaphors"; for instance, solidarity, common life, and shared concerns. It is a worthy ambition, Amin proposes, to want to "foster empathy between strangers," but a "politics of care for the stranger" may not appeal to many, and the answer is to "turn to other sites of conciliation and integration."[33] Making a similar argument from a different disciplinary perspective, theatre scholar Janelle Reinelt has suggested that theatre in the twenty-first century faces the challenge of the "ethical dimension of a new global perception," having to face up to "how increased inter-connectedness entails substantial obligations and alliances between previously discrete or even exclusive ideas of citizenship, ethnicity and affiliation."[34]

Nightmare/Dream and *The Global Savages* both contribute fresh metaphors and uncertain terms of encounter, and thus stage strangers in such a way that calls up a meaningful encounter with difference. They stage a meaningful encounter with difference though immersion or participation and, in a gentle fashion, allow space for the difficult and indeterminate. This is not to say that these examples are generalizable models to be emulated; nor do I mean to suggest with this final chapter that poetic realist plays are incapable of forming meaningful relationships to distant strangers. There is, as I wrote in my Introduction, no "correct" or perfectly portable means of activating an audience. It is to say that, while a moral melodrama affirms its audience's pre-existing opinions and worldviews, these examples allow the audience to imagine themselves into a more dynamic and fluid encounter with difference where the outcome is uncertain. They represent the legacies of colonialism to complexly stage the stranger as both included or excluded, at the threshold of the present moment of encounter. Both performances walk a fine line to neither alienate their audiences from history, nor accuse them of moral complacency; nor do they have their audiences congratulate themselves on having overcome the material challenges still facing those marked as strangers today. They are two examples among many others representing a pendulum swing toward theatrical poetics and practices that interweave the aesthetic and the relational, the represented and the "real," and which offer something more than cloying appeals to empathy with strangers and a patronizing politics of care.

There are multiple arguments today for a failure of representation, or at least a failure of what representation can achieve alone, and a shift away from a moral poetics toward a poetics that is more disruptively or unpredictably ethical. Applying Levinas's philosophy to performance in Australia, Tom Burvill notes how refugee performances there exhibit a similar dissatisfaction. "It is not so much the characters' struggle with moral dilemmas, so central to the traditions of serious European drama, that is the issue here," writes Burvill. "It is more a matter of how the experience of 'being there' interpolates the audience, what it 'does to you' to be present at the event of the performance, in terms of the encounter with alterity."[35] This may be part of a widespread increasing emphasis in the production of liveness itself,[36] what Lehmann calls the "cultural phenomenon of the production of presence" which, in opposition to the mimesis of representation, is "gaining in importance."[37] If the performances I have discussed in this chapter are an indication of the need for new poetics of encounter, then they point the way to a richer, more inventive, and more uncertain mode of representation than Lehmann's postdramatic theatre. They also illustrate that the ethical need not require, as it does for Lehmann, that theatre transgress social norms or confront its audience. Lehmann writes of a "politics of perception" because the aesthetic he is responding to prioritizes visual theatrical signs; however, the paths by which theatre finds its way to a difficult and indeterminate ethics are many. In *Nightmare/Dream* it is by way of a kaleidoscopic drifted subjectivity and the associated denial of any fixed or privileged positions of witness; in *The Global Savages* it is by way of attention to the intersubjective, social relations of the whole performance encounter and the blurred line between the real and the represented, as well as the group's taking ownership over the making strange of its own exoticized image.[38]

One of the questions I set out to answer for myself with this book was: What is it that Canadian theatre might contribute to a global ethics, that is, to meaningfully seeing, knowing, or caring for strangers in a globalized, twenty-first-century context? Among the myriad ways we might bear witness, or learn about others, or be propelled to empathy or action, what might be the special contribution theatre can make? These examples demonstrate such diverse aesthetic strategies that the answer clearly does not lie any preferred dramaturgy or in any preferred means of "activating" the audience. Ultimately, what I think theatre is helping sort out is something Nicholas Ridout discusses in his *Theatre and Ethics* as the ethical implications of "being there."[39] He writes that "being there" means at least three things: "first, simply to be present, to attend, as at the theatre; to be there is, second, to be part of it, to participate, as in politics, for example; and finally, to be there is to be there for someone to engage in a relationship of care or support, to accept an ethical responsibility for the other." Ridout then adds the critical questions: "Did you have to be there?" and "Is being there enough?"[40] What the examples of *Nightmare/Dream* and *The Global Savages* offer as an answer is that performance can offer a ethical encounter with strangers that scrutinizes the very way strangers are staged in the encounter. In the examples in this chapter, this meant being able to quite literally expose differentials of power, the material forces that create or maintain the stranger's strangeness, or historical conditions that haunt the present moment. By making the rules visible, ethical encounter may make them negotiable as well. What has the stranger's "being there" meant, and what has it meant for the audience to "be there" with them? As Ridout writes, "being there" may not "be enough," particularly when what it means to "be there" has been too fully calculated prior to the encounter.

If, as I argued in my opening chapter, meaningful ethical encounter in theatre is fundamentally a matter of presenting meaningful choices to be made, then theatre's turn toward participatory and relational modes of engaging audiences is a positive development. But it will be important to remain critical about what choices are available, what they mean, and who gets to decide. Choice means more than the choice about whether or not – as in *A Taste of Empire* – to take a single symbolic action. There is the choice to determine what presence has meant, the choice to be willing to adopt multiple or even conflicting perspectives, or the choice to see how choice itself is layered over with the sediments of history, politics, and power. And what seems to be the case in *Nightmare/Dream* and *The Global Savages* is that the strangers themselves have a choice, a choice to be something other than a mirror in which the dominant culture might see itself, a choice to be there on their own terms.

EPILOGUE

Stranger Danger

I write this epilogue a day following "Brexit," the United Kingdom's decision to exit the European Union as a result of its 23 June 2016 referendum. The fallout of this seismic political event has barely begun, but it includes nothing less than the renewed possibility of Scottish independence and the unification of Ireland. The most chilling aspect of the referendum's outcome is that it represents the first real victory in the West in a major vote of an openly nationalist, anti-immigrant, even xenophobic political campaign. As I write, there is grave concern that the same politics will serve Donald Trump in his candidacy for US president in the 2016 election.

Brexit and Trump – along with the rising profile of far right parties in Europe such as Greece's Golden Dawn or France's National Front – may, terrifyingly, be the coming to a rolling boil of what has been a slowly simmering populist xenophobia in the West. This trend, observable around the world during the time I wrote the bulk of this book, underscores the need for the careful ethics of difference I have argued for in these pages. It was observable in many of the newsworthy events that took place throughout 2014 and 2015 as I wrote. In November 2014 here in Canada, for example, Michael Zehaf-Bibeau, a Libyan-Canadian man who had been living in a homeless shelter in Ottawa, shot and killed a young Canadian soldier named Nathan Cirillo at the National War Memorial and went on to storm the Parliament buildings before being gunned down by security guards. In the weeks following the event, the government and much of the media worked the tragic incident up into a larger narrative of fear and anxiety about a looming threat of violence fuelled by Islamic extremism. Zehaf-Bibeau had been professing allegiance to ISIS online, but the narrative of a large terror threat to Canada disregarded the extreme rarity of such events in the country. The media's contortions of reality even led to a completely invented story (which was later retracted) that a video Zehaf-Bibeau had recorded included an exhortation to others to carry out similar attacks.[1] A stranger living a troubled life at the threshold of Canadian society, Zehaf-Bibeau, through his horrible act, became a villain in the public narrative – not a neighbour for whom a community might bear some collective responsibility, but an other who was indelibly marked as monstrous, foreign, and representative of a looming catastrophe. It became clear that the sitting Conservative government's agenda of making Zehaf-Bibeau a bogeyman of Western civilization was to build public support for its Bill C-51, legislation granting the government greater powers of surveillance.

Several months later in the spring of 2015 and halfway across the world, a boat full of migrants seeking passage to Europe sank off the coast of Libya, an estimated seven hundred of them drowning before they could be reached by rescue ships. The incident was only one particularly spectacular example of a recurring tragedy on a body of water on which unknown numbers of people lose their lives fleeing war, disease, famine, or abject poverty.[2] The international media's reportage kept these strangers at the threshold by calling them "migrants" or "stowaways" instead of refugees (given that the latter term becomes a claim on human rights). Reports also kept these strangers nameless, faceless, dehistoricized and de-particularized. Just as depicted in *The Sheep and the Whale*, which was inspired twenty years ago by just such stories in that part of the world, the migrants had to forget where they were from, burn their passports, and drown their past, presumably as the "price" of admission to the "first world." The images that circulated of the incident were long shots taken at a distance of boats overflowing with masses of faceless brown and black human bodies, a uniform mob on the verge of sinking the boat, and perhaps by extension, as the Western media would have it, Europe along with it. In the fall of 2015, this abstract de-personalization of the refugees in the media would be interrupted by the now-famous image of Alan Kurdi, a three-year-old Syrian boy whose body was photographed washed up on the Turkish shore; in Canada, the image propelled an outpouring of support that played a part in the defeat of the Conservative government of Stephen Harper. Back in the UK earlier that year, a hateful diatribe in a British tabloid suggested the migrants were like cockroaches and that the boats should be approached with military rather than rescue ships.[3] The backlash to the piece was intense, but the fact that it was ever published bore testament to the simmering feelings that the United Kingdom Independence Party stoked during the Brexit Leave campaign, most infamously by means of a controversial poster showing a long line of refugees with the headline, "Breaking Point."[4]

These examples demonstrate a renewed climate of what Zygmunt Bauman speaks of as "stranger danger," the attitude whereby strangers, whether migrants, immigrants, or refugees, become the "collateral damage" of modernity, deprived of the opportunity of a safe and decent life, and deprived again of inclusion in the human community even in their deaths by acts of making strange. As Luc Boltanski has suggested, the media often use such events in an ongoing "spectacle of misery" that is in fact deliberately crafted to dis-incentivize spectators to care or act.[5] In these examples distant strangers catapult into public consciousness through spectacular tragedy, as visible in their suffering as they were invisible before it. The slowly surfacing and dangerous anger that results from this easy projection of social ills onto immigrants, foreigners, refugees, even the failing "elites," sets tremendously high stakes for staging strangers today.

This book is the culmination of a research project that began a decade ago in my doctoral studies. The aim of this work has been to cut through a celebratory discourse about encounter with difference in theatre in order to be alive both to its possibilities and to its hazards. The contribution I hope to have made to that ongoing project with this book is to have deepened the conversation about difference in performance by providing fresh language and critical points of reference. My critical framework, including such notions as a distinction between moral and ethical modes of address, the metaphor of the stranger, and my takes on the discourses of multiculturalism and global ethics have been meant to build a case for a theatre that can powerfully confront the critical ethical problems of the cultural moment. I have expressed concerns about how theatre may exoticize or domesticate strangers in undesirable ways and pointed out how discourses surrounding theatre may appeal to spurious notions of seeing, knowing, and caring for strangers. All of this arose from a skepticism fuelled in the early days of this project by Bauman's wish to see past a superficial knowing that may result from ethical encounter:

> On the whole, in most daily encounters, in most modalities of being together, we manage to understand each other in the Wittgensteinian sense of understanding, of "knowing how to go on," to cope with the task of sorting out right, adequate or passable responses to each other's moves, even though an analyst would find that understanding wanting, incomplete or illusory, the illusion being caused by habituated and mutually tolerated routines of avoidance rather than the sharing of meanings.[6]

Theatre – a place some may love for its convention and ritual – is likewise susceptible to routines of avoidance. It does not, however, necessarily take an "analyst" to find either daily or representational encounters with difference lacking. The practices of ejection and domestication, for instance, are sometimes near to the surface, and the trade-offs of the stranger's fraught appearance are evident to some – if not always to all – parties to an encounter.

In addition to working up a skeptical perspective on ethics, I hope the book has also demonstrated positive ways in which strangers positioned at the threshold often exhibit a kind of psychic dual citizenship that can challenge calcified or stagnant notions of community. In chapter 2, for instance, I laid out how the strangers of the nonprofessional culturally focused theatre maintained an active globalism in spite of a nationalistic multicultural discourse that positioned their work as folklore. I suggested in chapter 3 how the generational family drama may make strangers safe in a way that avoids difficult questions about the present, but proposed as well that, in a globalized context, these dramas are also staging important choices being made within families as one "near sphere of moral concern." In chapter 4, I observed that while melodrama and the white-knight narrative may overindulge the victimization of the witness, and by extension that of the witnessing audience, we may nonetheless find in them an undeniable contemporary longing for "moral legibility" (even if one to approach with caution). Finally, in chapter 5, I refused to automatically accept the ethical potential of supposedly more "active" audiences, pointing to a need to think expansively about how an audience's relationship to the stranger may be continually and freshly imagined.

The book's central conceit of "the stranger" allows for a view of difference not as an immutable marker of identity but as an assigned role that is socially constructed in relation to local communities, to nation, to multicultural policy, and to notions of global ethics. Influenced strongly by Sara Ahmed's *Strange Encounters*, I turned my thinking toward the question of how markers of difference in representation and the discursive practices surrounding them become mechanisms for social differentiation. Such social negotiation of difference may well be turned either to a positive end – as in a complex encounter in performance that offers a kaleidoscopic perspective on the legacy of colonialism through intersubjective encounter among performers and spectators; or to a negative end – as in stories of the white knight that generate suffering witnesses to the detriment of suffering victims. Through developing more refined discussions of difference, we can become more conscious about who is made strange and to what end. Agreeing that "groups are made strange by the active intervention of interpreting subjects," Jeffrey C. Alexander warns of the possibility that "intellectuals, political leaders, and ordinary persons alike move to create a division between 'us' and 'them.'"[7] The kind of benign strangeness that Georg Simmel imagined in his cosmopolitan nineteenth-century Berlin seems as ready as it ever was in history to become a terrible and violent form of exclusion. Ash Amin is right to point out that contemporary xenophobia may occasion a reconsideration of the multicultural critiques of the 1990s; as much as multiculturalism may have been "smug in assuming the authority to grant rights to the 'deserving' stranger," it did not "condone a culture of vigilantism and punishment," propelled by the culture of stranger danger.[8]

In closing, I offer two surprising and useful insights I have had during this project. The first is that, while the clean distinction I drew out in chapter 1 between moral and ethical modes provides useful language, its application to specific contexts of encounter gets considerably messier when sustained reflection makes multiple, ambivalent, and often more generous, readings available. As I went along I began to look differently at number of situations that, in the early stages of writing, I had held up as examples of ejection or domestication of the stranger. It became clear over time that, rather than cling to distinctions between the moral and ethical, I needed to make room in my commentary for the difficulty and indeterminacy that I was arguing for in theatre. It became important to say, for instance, that while Herbert Whittaker may have made comments that folklorized nonprofessional culturally focused theatre, his reviews could also be understood as part of a tradition of Canadian theatre criticism, and that his work drew attention to the nonprofessional theatre in a way that few critics did then or have since. The generational family drama may well be prescriptively moral in its positioning of an ancestral culture in a "primordial" past, but, at the same time, it also makes public the private experience of first- and second-generation immigrant women in Canada. The growing canon of white-knight stories may cumulatively be creating an audience positioned on "high moral ground," but these stories are individually well meaning and their "thematic ethics" and predictable reflexivity may nonetheless be preferable to their complete absence. Keeping these arguments in tension has been a meta-lesson in ethics as process, and as something requiring space, time, and most of all, an open-minded attention, to unfold. Beyond being a personal lesson in needing time for myself to "get it right," I think this also suggests a need for deeper thinking about the conventional time-structures of encounter in performance events, and about how subtle and more contradictory meanings sometimes only become available after the ready-made ones are revealed and set aside.

A related surprising insight was the discovery that in discussing the ethics of staging strangers I was necessarily discussing audiences, both in the sense of individual viewing subjects and as a viewing "public" that constitutes larger "circles of the 'we,'" including the multicultural nation, the West, or humanity. This discovery perhaps allows for a more generous reading of my example of *The Stranger* from the Prologue to the book. If *The Stranger* reduced strangers to conventional markers of identity, rather than to examples of a strange and challenging alterity,[9] its holding up a mirror to the audience foreshadowed the many examples of staging strangers throughout the book that implied particular viewing subjects. In short, a book about ethics became a book about audiences in a way I had not anticipated (I recently arrived at this insight in reverse at a conference on the theme of theatre and spectatorship, which ended up being heavily focused on ethics). Although it was not an original part of my design, this change in perspective may end up being one of this book's important contributions to the discussion of encounter with difference in theatre. As I suggested in chapter 1, the tradition of intercultural discourse, influenced as it was historically by European formalism, has paid almost exclusive attention to the emancipatory qualities of *representation*, which, through its mixing of cultural "signs," creates counter-hegemonic political and cultural meanings. *Staging Strangers* has instead adopted a view of performance as *encounter,* as a meeting of subjectivities and collectivities coded, if never wholly determined, by discourses of difference.

The fact that audience became an important focus of the book ultimately exposes perhaps its chief limitation: its dependence on my individual perspective as a witnessing and interpreting subject who was only able to speculate about how others might imagine themselves into an encounter. Without discounting the validity of first-person accounts – my doctoral research about intercultural theatre adopted an ethnographic methodology – such information could be usefully corroborated or challenged by qualitative and empirical research into how spectators makes meaning out of encounters with difference. If the book has explored how theatre might contribute meaningfully to the development of a more ethical public, then such research might profitably attend as well to the conventions and practices surrounding performance that shape how its interventions enter the public sphere. I am thinking here not just of the textual discursive practices of reviews or scholarly writing, or of online commentary on blogs and social media, though all of these play a role. I am thinking of the lived practices and rituals of the theatre, of the way audiences are called on within and immediately after performance to make sense of their experience. Typical formats for immediate response, post-show Q & A sessions or "talk backs," tend to be occasions to rehearse the most familiar and safe ideas or to perform the expected reactions according to unspoken social protocols. Rarely is the uncomfortable or the unsavoury broached, and more rarely still is the moment of interpretation historicized to show how it is set upon by layers of history, power or cultural politics. And, if one is interested in meaningful ethical encounters with difference: do post-show sessions and panels that ask for an immediate, rational intellectualization of the work not deaden performance's salient and unique powers to unsettle, to disturb, to make layered and complex, to occasion a seeing and knowing that is felt, intuitive, or embodied? A key insight of a recent large, empirical study of audiences carried out in the UK by the British Theatre Consortium and led by Janelle Reinelt[10] was that in the immediate wake of a performance, spectators placed value on theatre's "liveness" and "sensual immediacy,"[11] whereas in the weeks following, they more greatly valued "theatre's opportunity to generate ideas and debate" (with the earlier, less effable values dropping off the list).[12] How might we differently configure bodies in a room to blend the work of representation and dialogue such that these two knowledges, however partial, uncomfortable, and inarticulate, might find a different path into individual understanding and thereby into public discourse? And how, to answer a call Matthew Reason has recently issued, might our interpretative practices move beyond "over-statements of idealized or imagined possibilities" to consider how *actual* audiences "engage with the different invitations to participate offered by contemporary theatre and performance"?[13] How might such encounters be thought of not as extraneous – and probably pre-emptive – acts of intellectualization, but as part of an ethical meta-design (or an interruptive "anti-design"?) in which the spaces of representation and social interaction blur and where new knowledge may more slowly and organically emerge?

Last of all, I hope the book has made clear the need for a difficult and indeterminate ethics. That is not so easy precisely because the fact that we live in such uncertain times exerts a gravitational pull toward the certain. Still, if Bauman is correct in saying that it is a "newly perceived impotence that makes our uncertainty feel more ghastly and menacing than before,"[14] the solution is not to rush to certainty, nor to let a legitimate outrage congeal too easily into an "us" and a "them," nor to settle for too long into fixed ways of seeing or knowing. In an interview about her book *The Fragility of Goodness: Luck and Ethics in Greek Tragedy and Philosophy*, Martha Nussbaum expresses what she has learned from reading Greek dramas:

> To be a good human being is to have a kind of openness to the world, an ability to trust uncertain things beyond your own control, that can lead you to be shattered in very extreme circumstances for which you were not to blame. That says something very important about the human condition of the ethical life: that it is based on a trust in the uncertain and on a willingness to be exposed; it's based on being more like a plant than like a jewel, something rather fragile, but whose very particular beauty is inseparable from its fragility.[15]

Nussbaum's eloquent call to embrace uncertainty, inspired by a profoundly ethical theatre tradition more than two millennia ago, serves well as a closing wish for theatre makers and their audiences alike in the new millennium.

Notes

PROLOGUE

1 *The Stranger* was restaged as part of the Summerworks Festival a year later in 2015, and again in September 2016, each time with some of the same characters and scenes described here.

2 This book focuses on "cultural" representation, but with an awareness that "culture" necessarily implies dimensions of belonging and difference such as race, ethnicity, and nationality, each of which carries its own conceptual and historical baggage, and none of which are mutable in the same ways. To avoid any awkward repetition of such a list throughout, however, I use "cultural difference," or simply "difference," as shorthand and make clear where these other dimensions become important to the discussion. Also, although I drop the quotation marks around such terms as "stranger" and "strange" after these initial mentions, in my analysis I discuss the many ways in which these are performative discursive constructions rather than any inherent and fixed "foreignness."

3 Levinas, *Totality and Infinity* or Bauman, *Strangers at Our Door*. For an example of how the stranger might be discussed in other ways in the context of social or public performance, see Butler, *Frames of War* or Phelan, *Sexual Strangers*.

4 The essay is translated and reprinted in Wolfe, *Georg Simmel*, 402.

5 Wolfe, *Georg Simmel*, 402.

6 Kearney and Semonovitch, *Phenomenologies*, 3.

7 Wolfe, *Georg Simmel*, 403.

8 Rumford, *Globalization*, 7.
9 Ibid., 8.
10 Ibid.
11 Ibid., 22.

CHAPTER ONE

1 "Mandate," *Cahoots Theatre Company*, http://www.cahoots.ca/about/mandate/
2 Vit Wagner, "Cahoots Zeroing in on 'Workshop Ghetto,'" *Toronto Star*, 11 November 1993.
3 Because this shift toward the global can be observed across Canada, I use the term "Canadian theatre" to describe the general field of practice across which I am speaking in this book. As I go on to point out, I focus on examples from Toronto. Also, I do not address the cultural politics of difference between Anglo and Franco Canada, nor in any substantial way how the politics and ethics of "intercultural" theatre play out uniquely in Quebec.
4 I borrow this phrase from James Overton's excellent book *Making a World of Difference,* a discussion of cultural myth, narrative, and economic underdevelopment in Newfoundland (where the phrase appears on vehicle license plates). See Overton, *Making a World.*
5 Doucet, "Anatomy," 9.
6 For example, see Reuters, "Toronto Still 'Younger One' among World's Major Multicultural Cities: Professor," *National Post*, 28 December 2007; or Francine Kopun and Nicholas Keung, "A City of Unmatched Diversity; Many Newcomers Opt to Bypass City, Start New Lives in Suburbs Surrounding Toronto," *Toronto Star*, 5 December 2007.
7 Doucet, "Anatomy," 7.
8 McKinnie, "Performing the Civic," 112–13.
9 "Creative Capital Gains: An Action Plan for Toronto," *City of Toronto,* http://www.livewithculture.ca/wp-content/uploads/2011/05/CCI-Final.pdf.
10 Jim Byers, "TO-Bid's Pitch: 'Expect the World'; Olympic Group Hopes to Stir Excitement Olympic Officials Unveil a Slogan – and a Festive Logo," *Toronto Star*, 12 April 2000.
11 "Panamania Toronto 2015," http://www.toronto2015.org/panamania.

12 Matthew Trevisan, "Toronto Can Position Itself as a First-Tier Mega-Region," *Globe and Mail*, 7 July 2007.

13 "Insight: Creative and Diverse: Ranking Global Cities," *Martin Prosperity Institute*, http://martinprosperity.org/global-cities/Global%20Cities_000%20Scorecard%20Grades.pdf.

14 "Project: Global Cities Index," *Martin Prosperity Institute*, http://martinprosperity.org/ projects/project-global-cities-index/.

15 Myungsook Lee, "Diversity in Canadian Workplaces," *Diverse Magazine*, http://diversemagazine.ca/Culture-diversity&workplace.htm.

16 See, for instance, a National Angus Reid Poll in 1992 and another conducted by Leger Marketing in 2007 that focused on racism in Quebec and generated controversy. A larger study was designed in 2003 by the Centre for Research and Information on Canada, the *Globe and Mail*, and the Canadian Opinion Research Archive; see Andrew Parkin and Matthew Mendelsohn, "A New Canada: An Identity Shaped by Diversity," *Centre for Research and Information on Canada*, http://www.multiculturalmentalhealth.ca/wp-content/uploads/2014/01/cric-gmnc-03-not_000.pdf.

17 "Quarterly Activity Report: 3rd Quarter 2014," *Housing Connections*, http://www.housingconnections.ca/PDF/QuarterlyReports/2014/Quarterly%20 Activity%20Report%20-%20Q3%202014.pdf.

18 See the City of Toronto's "Wellbeing Project" website for direct access to this data, but for a helpful series of visualizations of the data see David Topping, "Toronto's Most, and Least, Diverse Neighbourhoods," *The Grid*, 6 December 2012.

19 Knowles, *How Theatre Means*, 5.

20 Massey, "Possibilities of a Politics," 412.

21 Massey, *World City*, 166.

22 Ibid., 193.

23 Mark Ravenhill, "Edinburgh Festival Speech: 'We Need to Have a Plan B,'" *The Guardian*, 3 August 2013.

24 Banting and Kymlicka, "Canadian Multiculturalism," 50.

25 Taylor, *Multiculturalism*, 25.

26 Peer Shouten, "Theory Talks #43: Saskia Sassen on Sociology, Globalization, and the Re-shaping of the National," *Theory Talks*, http://www.theory-talks.org/2011/09/theory-talk-43.html.

27 Thobani, *Exalted*, 149.

28 Ahmed, *Strange Encounters*, 99.
29 Žižek, "Multiculturalism," 17.
30 Amin, *Land of Strangers*, 3.
31 Rumford, *Globalization*, 1.
32 The phrases "non Anglo or Franco," "culturally marked," and "visible minorities" all call up particular associations and values, and each is dissatisfying for its own reason: "non Anglo or Franco" positions those settler European cultures as dominant and legitimate; "culturally marked" is versatile and innocuous but also suggestive of an indelible identification; "visible minorities," the term long-used in government, implies that "visible" difference is what counts. The term "intercultural" is more neutral and has likely proven popular for that reason. But striving for neutrality in a discussion that is pursuing "difficult" ethical encounters with difference may not be desirable either; as Žižek's writes, "the struggle for ideological and political hegemony is thus always the struggle for the appropriation of terms which are 'spontaneously' experienced as 'apolitical,' as transcending political boundaries" (Žižek, "Multiculturalism," 30). Also, because the "intercultural" points to mixing, it seems peculiar to identify individuals or communities as "intercultural," particularly in cases where they are invested in constituting their wholeness (and for this reason, "multicultural" becomes the appropriate term in chapter 2). My choice is to use the phrase most appropriate to each context and to have the discussion unpack problems manifest in the language.
33 Appadurai, *Modernity at Large*, 19.
34 Bharucha, "Politics of Culturalisms," 486.
35 Ibid., 487.
36 Appiah, *Ethics of Identity*, 110.
37 Ibid., 107.
38 "Authenticity" is itself a spurious notion for Appiah because cultural artifacts and traditions are always, when traced back far enough, the products of some other culture, somewhere else. Appiah holds up intercultural "contamination" as a positive counter-value. See Appiah, "Case for Contamination."
39 Eagleton, *Trouble with Strangers*, 245.
40 Ibid., 83.
41 Ibid., 24.

42 Some representative examples: Emmanuel Levinas was a Russian-Lithuanian Jew who lived most of his life in France; Zygmunt Bauman was a Polish Jew who fled the Nazis, ended up first in the Soviet Union, and later took up a position at the University of Leeds in the UK, where he had a successful scholarly career writing in English, his third language; Sara Ahmed was born to a Pakistani father and British mother in England and is now based in Australia; Saskia Sassen grew up in Argentina with Dutch parents, speaks five languages, and now teaches in the United States and the UK; Kwame Appiah is London-born and American-educated, but grew up in and maintains close ties to the Asante area of Ghana; Arjun Appadurai was raised and trained in India and is now on faculty at the New School in New York; Rustom Bharucha is based in Kolkata but has professional affiliations in Europe and the United States; and Cambridge professor Ash Amin is a Ugandan-born British academic who has lived and worked in Italy, Denmark, the Netherlands, and Sweden.

43 Bauman, *Liquid Modernity*, 47.

44 Ibid., 48.

45 Ibid., 39.

46 Since the notion of the "public sphere" was popularized by the German philosopher Jurgen Habermas in the 1960s and 1970s, many have pointed to its lacunae. See, for instance, Nancy Fraser, "Global Justice and the Renewal of Critical Theory," http://www.eurozine.com/articles /2009-04-21-fraser-en.html; or Hardt and Negri, *Empire*; or Negt, *Public Sphere*.

47 Bauman, *Community*, 78.

48 Ibid., 80.

49 Bauman and Bauman, *Culture*, 46.

50 Nancy Fraser, quoted in Bauman, *Community*, 77.

51 Zygmunt Bauman, "The Changing Nature of Work and Agency in Times of Interregnum," *Social Europe*, 9 January, 2014, http://www.socialeurope.eu/2014/01/interregnum/.

52 Bauman, *Liquid Modernity*, 76.

53 Ibid., 35.

54 Knowles, *Reading*, 146.

55 Ibid.

56 Giddens, *Runaway World*, 3.

57 Castells, *End of Millennium*, 1 2.

58 McKinnie, *City Stages*, 10–11.
59 Gilbert and Lo, *Performance and Cosmopolitics*, 13.
60 For more on this distinction, see Schellekens, 68–71 or Ella Peek, "Ethical Criticism of Art," *The Encyclopedia of Philosophy*, http://www.iep.utm.edu/art-eth/.
61 Ridout, *Theatre and Ethics*, 9.
62 Nussbaum, *Fragility*, 83.
63 Ibid., 13.
64 King, *Ethos of Drama*, 3.
65 Ibid., 27.
66 Rumford, *Globalization*, 3.
67 Ibid., 7.
68 I return to this problem in my Epilogue and cite a recent empirical study of audiences. Also, two doctoral students at the Centre for Drama, Theatre and Performance Studies in Toronto are currently conducting extensive qualitative studies of audiences: Jenny Salisbury, whose work is considering how audiences relate to community-based performance, and Scott Mealey, who is conducting empirical research into how theatre "persuades" its audiences to adopt particular points of view.
69 Davis, *Art and Politics*, 50–1.
70 Kitcher, *Ethical Project*, 2.
71 Ibid., but also Trout, *The Empathy Gap*.
72 See Singer et al. or Gutsell and Inzlicht, "Empathy Constrained."
73 See Ornstein, *New World New Mind*.
74 See Kahneman and Tversky, "Prospect Theory."
75 See Slovic, "If I Look at the Mass"; but also Lifton, *Death in Life* – with whom the idea is most associated.
76 For an outline of the arguments emerging from contemporary psychological and cognitive research as they relate to theatre, see Freeman, "Social Neuroscience."
77 See Pinker, *The Better Angels*.
78 Hardt and Negri, *Empire*, xv.
79 Ibid., 23–4.
80 Ibid., 48.
81 Singer, *One World*, 172.
82 Ibid., 13.
83 Bauman, *Liquid Modernity*, 199.

84 Rae, "Cosmopolitan Stage," 11.
85 Boltanski, *Distant Suffering*, 20.
86 Wolfe, *Georg Simmel*, 406.
87 Rumford, *Globalization*, 6.
88 I use the term "nonprofessional" to avoid the stigmatized term "amateur," and my unhyphenated use follows that of Canadian theatre historian Robin C. Whittaker, whose work has focused on the nonprofessional sector. I use "culturally focused" to avoid other problematic terms such as ethnic theatre, immigrant theatre, multicultural theatre, and even "ghetto" theatre.
89 These characteristics, to be expanded upon in chapter 4, are derived from Brooks.

CHAPTER TWO

1 Ahmed, *Strange Encounters*, 95.
2 Filewod, "Erasing Historical Difference," 207.
3 Wolfe, *Georg Simmel*, 402.
4 See note in chapter 1 about my use of this term.
5 The discussion makes it necessary to use a shorthand – "dominant culture" – to describe the culture that is *not* culturally marked. Given that the dominant culture itself is being slowly reshaped in this historical moment in Canada, I acknowledge the complexity this disguises, but nonetheless go on to identify the way that multiculturalism legitimizes culture marked as *not* multicultural.
6 Bryden and Neil, *Whittaker's Theatre*, ix.
7 Lo and Gilbert, "Toward a Topography," 33–4.
8 "Number and share of the foreign-born population in Canada, 1901 to 2006," *Statistics Canada*, http://www12.statcan.ca/census-recensement/2006/as-sa/97-557/figures/c1-eng.cfm.
9 Bauman, "Migration and Identities," 429.
10 "Toronto Facts: Diversity," *City of Toronto Website*, http://www1.toronto.ca/wps/portal/contentonly?vgnextoid=dbe867b42d853410VgnVCM10000071d60f89RCRD&vgnextchannel=57a12cc817453410VgnVCM10000071d60f89RCRD.
11 "2006 Census: Immigration in Canada: A Portrait of the Foreign-born Population," *Statistics Canada*, http://www12.statcan.ca/census-recensement/2006/as-sa/97-557/p24-eng.cfm.

12 "From Racism to Redress," *Canadian Race Relations Foundation*, http://www.crr.ca/divers-files/en/pub/faSh/ePubFaShRacRedJap.pdf.
13 Li, *Chinese in Canada*, 32.
14 See Tomovic, "Theatre among the Serbs," and Petroff, "Prosperity and Patriotism."
15 "Origin of the population, Census dates 1871–1971," *Statistics Canada*, http://www5.statcan.gc.ca/access_acces/archive.action?l=eng&loc=A125_163-eng.csv.
16 Wynnyckyj, "Amateur Theatre," 87.
17 Stefura, "Aspects of Culture," 32.
18 This list was assembled from a variety of sources but mainly from articles in the "Immigrant Theatre" issue of *Polyphony* cited throughout the chapter. Most dates were corroborated by multiple sources, but some, such as the Lithuanian or Finnish groups, depend on the veracity of single mentions in my sources.
19 Harney, "Ethnic Press," 1.
20 Herbert Whittaker, "A New Festival for Town Hall," *Globe and Mail*, 4 November 1972. 29.
21 Harney, "Immigrant Theatre," 3.
22 Lo and Gilbert, "Toward a Topography," 34.
23 Knowles, *Theatre & Interculturalism*, 69.
24 Robin Charles Whittaker, "Un/Disciplined Performance: Nonprofessionalized Theatre in Canada's Professional Era," (Thesis, 2012), https://tspace.library.utoronto.ca/handle/1807/32956.
25 "Czech" and "Slovak" in this chapter refer to two closely related nations and languages, joined in the single nation of Czechoslovakia between 1918 and 1992. My commentary in this chapter makes it necessary to sometimes speak of them as joined, sometimes separate. My discussion turns mainly to the Czech context on account of my knowledge of that country.
26 See Sayer, *Coasts of Bohemia.*
27 See Čermák, *Prince Rupert*.
28 The Benevolent Association helped persuade the Canadian government to admit twelve hundred refugees in 1968. Postwar exiles, worried about the fate of their country under the Soviets, lobbied influential Canadians to take notice. At one time, B.K. Sandwell, long-time editor of *Saturday Night,* was on the association's board of directors. According to Čermák, during the years of the Soviet Occupation "the associa-

tion spent countless hours trying to persuade the Canadian public and the Canadian government that Czechoslovakia deserved to be free," and thus it was that the association wrote into its mandate its purpose to "maintain and defend freedom and democracy in Canada." A longtime president of the association throughout the 1970s and '80s assisted directly in the work on the Canadian Multiculturalism Act (Čermák, *Prince Rupert*, 196–7).

29 Čermák, *Prince Rupert*, 19. For a full history of Masaryktown, see *Masaryktown: 50 Let Českého a Slovenského Národního Parku v Kanadě = 50 Years of Czech and Slovak National Park in Canada* (Toronto: Masaryk Memorial Institute, 1998).

30 This information about the history of Czech theatre in Canada, as well as that about the history of Nové divadlo, is derived from my discussions with longtime group participant Jana Fabiánová in the spring of 2013.

31 The Soviets, who had grown intolerant of the Czech's brand of liberal socialism under Alexander Dubček, invaded, seized and sealed the country tightly, bringing to an end the revival of a flourishing avant-garde movement across the arts in the interwar period when the Czech lands enjoyed a brief independence from external rule.

32 Vancouver has its own Czech and Slovak nonprofessional theatre company, Divadlo za rohem ("Theatre Around the Corner"), with a history comparable to that of Nové divadlo. See http://www.divadlozarohem.ca.

33 Safertal and Král, "It All Started with Adolf," 51.

34 Czech and Slovak organizations were formed to help ease the transition: the Masaryk Memorial Institute in Scarborough, the Czechoslovak National Council, the Czechoslovak Society of Arts and Sciences, SOKOL (the Czech sports and business organization), and *Spojené trampské osady*, "an ad hoc organization of outdoor enthusiasts who, in the tradition of Czech 'ramps' spent most of their weekends outdoors, camping and socializing around a bonfire" (Čermák, *Prince Rupert*, 52).

35 See Sayer, *Prague*.

36 "Odešel divadelník a exulant Adolf Toman," *Krajane.net*, http://krajane.net/article Detail.view?id=2324 (my translation).

37 Ray Conlogue, "Mame Reels along Rather Likeably," *Globe and Mail*, 16 September, 1980.

38 Goetz-Stankiewicz, *The Silenced Theatre*, 37.

39 Thobani, *Exalted Subjects*, 149.

40 Berger, "Coat of Many Colours," 223.

41 The MTAs arose in the wake of the decline of the Dominion Drama Festival (an organization that had promoted nonprofessional theatre for decades) and out of a debate about how to organize nonprofessional theatre in Canada generally, which by this time was being organized nominally and ineffectively by Theatre Canada. See Whittaker, "Undisciplined Performance," 220.

42 Off, "Heritage," 6.

43 The Ontario MTA originally formed in 1970 with six groups, and by 1985 had some sixty theatre companies, each operating in its own language. The amounts of money the MTAs received were always very modest compared to those going to mainstream institutions; even the NMTA only received about $70,000 in 1980, which was less than some individual – and new – theatre companies in Toronto received from the Toronto Arts Council alone (for instance Toronto Arts Productions, the precursor to today's Canadian Stage, received $75,000 in the same year, and the newly formed Young People's Theatre $95,000 – amounts that changed little in the subsequent decade). So despite the tiered organization and the rapidity with which it came about, the funding for these efforts was as shallow as it was broad, supporting the view that these initiatives were primarily motivated by politics. (See Di Giovanni, "Ontario Multicultural," and "Multicultural Groups Get Metro Grants," *Globe and Mail*, 2 May 1979.)

44 Herbert Whittaker, "Soldier Schweik Saga Splendidly Staged," *Globe and Mail*, 27 February 1969.

45 Whittaker, "Dramatic Exploration from Trinity Students," *Globe and Mail*, 12 February 1969.

46 Whittaker, "Laterna Magika Gets a New Lease on Life," *Globe and Mail*, 17 December 1977.

47 Whittaker, "Bright Hope from a Cultural Festival," *Globe and Mail*, 13 November 1972.

48 Burian, *Modern Czech Theatre*, 142.

49 Whittaker, "Festival Features Gifted Amateurs," *Globe and Mail*, 31 October 1973.

50 Hugh Winsor, "Want Own Department: Ethnic Groups Want More Funds, Programs," *Globe and Mail*, 17 October 1973.

51 John Dafoe, "Multiculturalism Could Do with Another Look," *Globe and Mail*, 17 November 1990.

52 Ibid.

53 Blaik Kirby, "Operetta Relies Heavily on One Singer," *Globe and Mail*, 29 November 1972.

54 Whittaker, "Earnest Amateurs Tackle Difficult Play," *Globe and Mail*, 6 November 1972.

55 By contrast, another major critic of the period, Urjo Kareda, paid essentially no attention to the nonprofessional culturally focused theatre despite himself being an immigrant to Canada from Estonia.

56 Kirby, "Operetta Relies Heavily on One Singer."

57 Ibid.

58 Whittaker, "White Nights Safe Bet for Start of Festival," *Globe and Mail*, 28 October 1974.

59 Whittaker, "New Wilde Farce Tricks Players," *Globe and Mail*, 20 October 1971.

60 John Fraser, "*Miss Julie*: Energetic but Superficial," *Globe and Mail*, 1 February 1973.

61 Robert Martin, "An Out-of-balance Moliere," *Globe and Mail*, 13 September 1972.

62 Harvie and Knowles, "Herbert Whittaker," 225.

63 This and all subsequent uncited details about Nové divadlo's history and productions were derived from research in the summer of 2013 in their uncatalogued archives held at the Masaryktown Memorial Institute in Scarborough, Ontario.

64 Wrote Michael Schonberg of V+W's influence: "The young generation of Czech artists and intellectuals who were principally responsible for the renaissance of Czechoslovakian theatre and of the cinema in the sixties freely admit their indebtedness to Voskovec and Werich." See Schonberg, *Osvobozené divadlo*, 4.

65 Nové divadlo, "25th Anniversary," 4 (Nové Divado, Toronto, 1994), my translation. In the years that followed, the group would perform several of Voskovec's plays from the interwar period, including *Slaměný Klobouk* (*Straw Hat*) in 1978, *Hej-Rup* (*Workers: Let's Go!*) in 1981, *V+W si pořádně zařádit* (*V+W Go Wild*) in 1982, and *Nebe na semi (Heaven and Earth)* in 1989.

66 Among Sixty-Eight's achievements was its publication of the first Czech edition of Milan Kundera's *Unbearable Lightness of Being* in 1985 nearly two decades before the famously translation choosy Kundera permitted another Czech version.

67 See Škvorecký, *Bůh do domu.*

68 Nové divadlo, program for *Bůh do domu* (Nové divadlo, Toronto, 1980), my translation.

69 Michal Schonberg translated and directed a student production at the University of Toronto Scarborough the previous year, and Vancouver's Kitsilano Theatre would produce the play in 1992.

70 Nové divadlo, "25th Anniversary"; my translation.

71 Ibid.

72 Associated Press, "Havel Meets a Legend," *Globe and Mail*, 24 Feb. 1990.

73 Immediately on his arrival, as if in a coronation, Toman became head of the 150-year-old Hálkovo městské divadlo Nymburk (Nymburk City Theatre), a post he held for twenty years, interrupted only by a two-year period when he was called to serve as the deputy minister of culture for the Czech Republic. For his work in Toronto, Toman would be awarded the Czech ministry of foreign affairs's Gratias Agit Award in 2010, for "spreading the good name of the Czech Republic internationally." For his work in Nymburk, the city would award him the honorific of the "Nymburk Lion." When Toman died of cancer in 2011, he was honoured at informal events in July at Toronto's Scotland Yard Pub on the Esplanade, and in September by the new owners of Limelight. See "Zemřela Nymburská Legenda, Divadelník Adolf Toman," *Nymburský Deník*, http://nymbursky.denik.cz/zpravy_region/toman_smrt20110717.html.

74 Král was an interesting figure himself: a political dissident in the early days of Communist rule who paid the price of a couple of years in prison in Prague. He found some solace in the company of Nové divadlo, and when Toman left, used his substantial administrative experience and the new possibilities for free travel after the revolution to build a vision for the theatre based on collaboration with Czech and Slovak professional actors.

75 Information in the following paragraphs about Nové divadlo productions and collaborations derives from their archives at Mararyktown, conversations with longtime group member Jana Fabiánová, and lists provided in the group's twenty-fifth anniversary pamphlet as well as in Safertal and Král, "It All Started with Adolf."

76 A clipping from the Czech magazine *Scena* in the Nové divadlo archives; my translation.

77 Notable guests of Nové divadlo include: Alena Bílková, Kamila Magálová, and Petr Kostka, all members of the Czech or Slovak national theatres; the famous Czech actor and folksinger Josef Zíma; and Stella Zázvorková, an actress who became known internationally for her role as mother to the protagonist of the Oscar-winning 1996 Czech film *Kolya.* Several times, the group invited Ladislav Smoljak, one of two members of the long-running quirky Czech comic theatre Járy Cimrmana (who, when I saw them in Brno in 2007 long after their heyday, still commanded a full house and rapturous applause), first in 1997 for the Cimrman play *Záskok* (*Double Cross*), with Smoljak himself playing the role of the main character, Prácheňský, and in 2004 to star in the Cimrman play *Švestka* (*Plum*). Other notable guest artists are the Vinohrady Theatre's Viktor Preiss, and Michal Dočolomanský, veteran of the Slovak National Theatre and father to Viliam Dočolomanský, now director of the widely celebrated experimental Czech theatre company *Farma v Jeskyni* (*Farm in a Cave*). In 1996 Král directed *Opala je poklad (Opala Is a Diamond)* by John Patrick with Jana Hlaváčová, "for many years the first lady of the National Theatre ensemble." In 2003 Hlaváčová and Petr Kostka would similarly reprise their roles in *Milostných dopisech (Love Letters)* from a Czech production at Vinohrady for Nové divadlo. In 1998 Slovak National Theatre actress Emília Vášáryová would perform in Bengt Ahlfors's *Divadelní komedie (A Theatre Comedy)*, which she would continue to perform in Slovakia at least until 2004. They would follow the same model in producing two pieces – *Boogie Boogie Gal* and *Holka nebo kluk* – by the musical theatre artist Antonín Procházka, nicknamed the "Molière of Plsen," and brought Procházka himself over to perform in both. Sources are various documents in the Nové divadlo archives, particularly its twenty-fifth anniversary pamphlet, corroborated as far as possible in my conversation with Jana Fabiánová and online.

78 Its production of Ladislav Stroupežnický's play *Naši furianti* (*Our Proud Peasants*), for example, was "modeled after the famous production of the Narodni divadlo, a taped recording of which was sent to us by Luděk Munzar," wrote Král. "Although the cast of the Nové divadlo has no actors comparable to the ensemble of the Prague theatre, the production was truly excellent, thanks to Machacek's superb treatment of the sets and Tomáš Mašek's impeccable direction." Their pro-

duction of Mamet's *Oleanna* in 2000 was styled after a 1999 production at the Slovak National Theatre. Safertal and Král, "It All Started with Adolf," 59.

79 For instance, Král himself wrote introductory scenes to *Nebe na zemi (Heaven on Earth)* and wrote a new adaptation of *Pest na ono (Fist in the Eye)*. Also, Brigitta Mavasová adapted for the stage Miloslav Švandrlík's book *Břetislav a Jitka* (Safertal and Král, "It All Started with Adolf," 61).

80 As in 2012, when the company presented an entirely original adaptation of Jan Neruda's *Malostranské Povídky*; or in 2013, when they augmented their production of Noel Coward's *Blithe Spirit* with original Czech songs by Lenda Nováková, Anthony Panacci, and Zdeněk Bruer.

81 Rut, "State of Czech Theatre," 290.

82 Appiah, *Politics of Culture*, 25.

83 Alexander, *Dark Side of Modernity*, 85.

84 See Berger, "Coat of Many Colours."

85 Mackey, *Random Acts of Culture*, 246.

86 Ian Willoughby, "Director Adolf Toman on Four Decades of Toronto's New Czech Theatre," *Radio Prague*, http://www.radio.cz/en/section/arts/director-adolf-toman-on-four-decades-of-torontos-new-czech-theatre.

87 Amin, *Land of Strangers*, 14.

88 Quoted in Bauman, *Liquid Modernity*, 191.

89 Till and Campbell, "Resistance Towards Ethics," 183 (my emphasis).

90 Janover, "Nostalgias," 117.

CHAPTER THREE

1 Ahmed, *Strange Encounters*, 57.

2 Ibid., 113.

3 Rewa, "Theatre & Ethnicity," 3.

4 Yhap, "Own Terms," 25.

5 Wolfe, *Georg Simmel*, 406.

6 Amin, *Land of Strangers*, 5.

7 Ibid., 2.

8 Ahmed, *Strange Encounters*, 94.

9 Li, "World Apart," 389.

10 For example, see Marc Maufort's gloss on the play in Maufort, *Transgressive Itineraries*, 107–10. Also, Jenna Rodgers has discussed how the light-

ing prescribed in the text to delineate the different characters' conflicted and politicized senses of space; see Rodgers, "Manipulating Theatrical Space."

11 See Giddens, *Modernity and Self-Identity.*

12 Papers from a 1993 conference at Lancaster University focusing on the "detraditionalization thesis" were published in Paul Heelas, Lash, and Morris, *Detraditionalization.*

13 Bauman, *Community*, 47.

14 See Giddens, *Runaway World.*

15 This was propelled particularly by the ascent of capitalism and industrialization, which combined to cleave discrete public and private realms, making the family a private sanctuary from various public social ills and corruptions (a pattern exploited to dramatic effect in the nineteenth-century stage melodramas discussed in chapter 4).

16 Quan, *Mother Tongue,* 29.

17 Ibid., 38.

18 Ibid., 19.

19 Ibid., 30.

20 Ibid., 31.

21 Ibid., 32.

22 Ibid., 28.

23 Lei, "Homeland under Attack," 36.

24 Ahmed, *Strange Encounters*, 79 (my emphasis).

25 Scott, *Nightwood Theatre*, 102.

26 Holledge and Tompkins, *Women's Intercultural*, 98.

27 Grosz's *chora* "is the space in which place is made possible, the chasm for the passage of spaceless Forms [sic] into a spatialized reality, a dimensionless tunnel opening itself to spatialization, obliterating itself to make others possible and actual." Grosz, *Space, Time, and Perversion*, 116.

28 Ibid.

29 Holledge and Tompkins, *Women's Intercultural*, 99.

30 Trask, *Globalization and Families*, 183.

31 Quan, *Mother Tongue*, 17.

32 Carlson, *Speaking in Tongues*, 20.

33 Quan, *Mother Tongue*, 37–8.

34 Ibid., 45.

35 Ibid., 36.

36 Ibid., 38.
37 Ibid., 48.
38 Ahmed, *Strange Encounters*, 88.
39 Hernandez, *Singkil*, 85.
40 Ibid., 95.
41 Ibid., 97.
42 Ibid., 95.
43 Ty, "Affect, Family," 219.
44 Bauman, *Liquid Modernity*, 65.
45 Intersectionality – a critical focus on intersecting forms of discrimination – was a feminist critical movement in the 1990s especially identified with sociologist Kimberlé Williams Crenshaw. See Crenshaw, "Mapping the Margins."
46 Trask, *Globalization and Families*, 195.
47 Hodkinson, *Female Parts*, 14.
48 Scott, *Nightwood Theatre*, 176.
49 Kaplan, "Manifest Domesticity," 582.
50 See DuBois, *Souls of Black Folk*.
51 Ahmed, *Strange Encounters*, 73.
52 Bauman, *Liquid Modernity*, 99.
53 "CBC Renews *Schitt's Creek* and *Murdoch Mysteries*, Cancels *Strange Empire*," http://www.cbc.ca/1.2979939.
54 Choi, *Kim's Convenience*, x.
55 J. Kelly Nestruck, "Kim's Convenience: Soft Drinks, Smokes, Family Dynamics," http://www.theglobeandmail.com/arts/theatre-and-performance/kims-convenience-soft-drinks-smokes-family-dynamics/article630504/
56 Joff Schmidt, "Kim's Convenience Rings up Heartfelt Laughs at Royal MTC," http://www.cbc.ca/news/canada/manitoba/kim-s-convenience-rings-up-heartfelt-laughs-at-royal-mtc-1.2572958.
57 Choi, *Kim's Convenience*, 28–31.
58 Ibid., 30.
59 Kamboureli, *Scandalous Bodies*, 83.
60 Massey, *World City*, 168.
61 Choi, *Kim's Convenience*, 19.
62 Ibid., vii.
63 Ibid., viii.
64 Bauman and Bauman, *Culture*, 69.

65 Quoted in Massey, "Possibilities of a Politics," 411.
66 Bauman, *Community*, 2.
67 Freeman, "Navigating," 64–6.
68 Ahmed, *Strange Encounters*, 69.
69 Quoted in Bauman, *Community*, 77.
70 Dolan, *Feminist Spectator*, 32.
71 Scott, *Nightwood Theatre*, 215.
72 Ouzounian, Richard. "Every Letter Counts is sincere and well-meaning but doesn't deliver," http://www.thestar.com/entertainment/stage/2013/01/31/every_letter_counts_is_sincere_and_wellmeaning_but_doesnt_deliver_review.html.
73 Cushman, Robert, "Factory's Every Letter Counts turns personal stories into misguided myths," http://news.nationalpost.com/arts/on-stage/theatre-review-factorys-every-letter-counts-turns-personal-stories-into-misguided-myths.
74 Bauman, *Does Ethics Have a Chance?* 28.
75 Appiah, "Cosmopolitan Patriots," 624.
76 Ibid.

CHAPTER FOUR

1 Razack, *Dark Threats*, 27.
2 Rae, "Cosmopolitan Stage?" 11.
3 Some other examples of plays structured around a protagonist's journey are *My Chernobyl* by Aaron Bushkowsky, *Afrika, Solo* by Djanet Sears, *The Peacemakers* by Natasha Greenblatt, Porte Parole's plays *Seeds* and *The Watershed*, Andrew Kushnir's *Small Axe* and *Wormwood*, and nearly all of Robert Lepage's productions.
4 Razack, *Dark Threats*, 26–7.
5 Glenn Sumi, "Powerful Politics," *NOW Toronto Magazine*, https://nowtoronto.com/stage /story.cfm%3Fcontent%3D138920.
6 Richard Ouzounian, "Weak Dialogue Undermines Bhopal Drama," *Toronto Star*, 24 October 2003.
7 Robert Cushman, "It's a Matter of Facts," *National Post*, 27 October 2003.
8 Barish, *Antitheatrical Prejudice*, 1.
9 Melodrama has its roots in the French Revolution. In the early nineteenth century, France was adjusting to a radically new liberal democra-

cy loosened from the authoritarianism and the certitude of life under monarchical rule. Melodrama was first realized in the novel, notably by Honoré de Balzac, and in the theatre, notably by Guilbert de Pixerécourt, the French playwright who wrote over a hundred plays for the Boulevards in Paris, who was wildly successful with audiences, and whose subsequent international fame helped spread what would become the conventions of melodrama throughout Europe and overseas. See Brooks, *Melodramatic*.

10 Brooks, *Melodramatic*, 11.

11 Ibid., 13.

12 Singer, *Melodrama and Modernity*, 134.

13 Brooks, *Melodramatic*, 12.

14 Varma, *Bhopal*, 15.

15 Ibid., 64.

16 See Smith, *Melodrama.*

17 Piketty compares brutal repressions of labour protests in the nineteenth and twenty-first centuries to illustrate the enduring conflict between rich and poor, owners of land and those who till it. The first two illustrations in the book offer a visualization of income levels in the United States and Europe from around the turn of the twentieth century to the turn of the twenty-first, and each reveals a clear "U-shape," showing high levels of inequality in the nineteenth century, dramatically lower levels in the mid–twentieth century, and a return, or a surpassing of nineteenth-century levels, over the last three decades. "In the Belle Époque," writes Piketty, "capital was king. In the years after World War II many people thought capitalism had been almost eradicated. Yet at the beginning of the twenty-first century Europe seems to be in the avant-garde of the new patrimonial capitalism, with private fortunes once again surpassing US levels." Piketty, *Capital*, 112.

18 Bauman, *Collateral Damage*, 8.

19 Brooks, *Melodramatic*, 15.

20 Ibid., 17.

21 Ibid., 56–80.

22 See Arendt, *On Revolution*.

23 Ibid., 86.

24 Appiah, *Experiments in Ethics*, 89.

25 Boltanski, *Distant Suffering*, 20.

26 Ibid., 13.

27 Wolfe, *Georg Simmel*, 406.
28 Ghazali, *Sheep*, 6.
29 Ibid., 53.
30 The play was initially inspired by a news story about people who had died in shipping containers aboard a cargo ship, and as well by the frequent dangerous passage of migrants on unsafe vessels, a global issue to which I return in the Epilogue.
31 Ibid., 8.
32 Ibid., 12.
33 Ibid., 23.
34 Ibid., 43.
35 Ibid., 44.
36 Ibid., 55.
37 Ibid., 21.
38 Writes Gluhovic: "*Homo sacer* represents bare life (literally one stripped of his or her humanity). An "obscure figure of archaic Roman law … *homo sacer* was the term used to describe a person who could be killed without punishment since he/she had been banished from the political-legal community and thus reduced to the status of bare physical existence." Gluhovic, "Too Distant Shores," 150.
39 Appiah, *Ethics of Identity*, 110.
40 Salverson, "Change," 124.
41 Ibid., 122.
42 In a separate essay reflecting on her own experience with students dealing with "tragic" subject matter, Salverson seeks out strategies to escape a melodramatic "gravitas" that seems to be expected both from the artists and the audience, finding, in her case, the physical technique of "clown" to provide one productive alternative. See Salverson, "Taking Liberties."
43 Their silence was made the more noticeable in the Theatre Passe Muraille production because the drowned refugees were played by youth who had participated in Cahoots's Crossing Gibraltar program – immigrant youth recruited into the cast to perform as the deceased and voiceless.
44 Ghazali, *Sheep*, 6. Ghazali's wish for the audience to feel uncomfortable is telling of his consciousness about the ethical implications of his aesthetic choices on his audience. The Theatre Passe Muraille production did manage to create this uncomfortable feeling with the lighting; the

play's Dora-nominated lighting design by Trevor Schwellnus amplified the sense of the stranger lurking in the shadows by means of tightly focused lights on actors peering out from behind pillars and cargo containers, their faces catching slivers of light in a visual metaphor of their longing for visibility. But Ghazali's hope that the containers would be imposing, "rise high up, creating an unpleasant feeling in the audience that they might fall on them at any given moment," was certainly not felt in the Passe Muraille production, where the containers were positioned at a comfortable and safe distance in a traditional proscenium setup.

45 Ghazali, *Sheep*, 23.

46 For the audience the characters, too, clearly divide into "goodies" and "baddies": the ship's captain is the Russian stereotype of a bullish, aggressive man, ignorant of the world, with colourful turns of phrase in a heavily accented English and dashes of racism and bigotry. He sees the drowned Africans is as merely an administrative inconvenience. His racist crew are cartoonish figures ripped from a Hollywood action film for their evil and ineptitude, hunting for the "nigger" stowaway as if he is a "half-dead rat." By contrast, the humanitarian Doctor is a similarly magnified figure of zealous devotion to the causes of saving stowaways and exposing the corruption cruelly manifesting around him, much like Dr Labonté in *Bhopal*.

47 Ghazali Ahmed, "Theatre and the Right of Interference," *Salabeckett.cat*, http://www.salabeckett.cat/files/pausa/extra-pausa/theatre-and-the-right-of-interference.-ahmed-ghazali.

48 Brooks, *Melodramatic*, 25.

49 Ibid., 42.

50 "KONY 2012," *YouTube* video, 29:58, Posted by Invisible Children, https://www.youTube.com /watch?v=Y4MnpzG5Sqc.

51 Martin Morrow, "Kony and the Birth of a New Stereotype: The Ugly Canadian," *Globe and Mail*, 29 March 2012.

52 The journey narrative is nearly ubiquitous in theatre dealing with global ethics, though it also appears in documentary plays as well; see Annabel Soutar's *Seeds* and *The Watershed*.

53 Pratt, *Imperial Eyes*, 5.

54 Razack, *Dark Threats*, 22.

55 Ibid., 25.

56 Hardt and Negri, *Empire*, 34.

57 Ibid., 36.

58 Ibid., 37.

59 The intense public backlash against *KONY 2012*, however, forced Invisible Children to respond, starting with their "Beyond Famous" video released a month following the first video. It is interesting that, in lieu of the argument of this chapter, the second video is narrated not by Russell but by another member of Invisible Children, Ben Keesy, and that it shows the many other people involved in the activist campaign. It was obviously calculated to correct the original video's focus on Russell as a journeying white knight. Unfortunately, this video was seen by only about 2 percent of the audience that saw the first video. See "KONY 2012: Part II – Beyond Famous," *YouTube* video, 19:47, posted by Invisible Children, https://www.youtube.com /watch?v=c_Ue6REkeTA.

60 MacKenzie, *SIA*, 67.

61 "Searching for *SIA* Part 1: Canada to Liberia," *YouTube* video, 7:40, Posted by Cahoots Theatre Company, https://www.youtube.com/watch ?v=3AXHrEW25G8.

62 Jason Russell, *Q*, by Jian Ghomeshi, 23 May 2013, https://www.cbc.ca/q/-russell-michael-c-hall-nigella-lawson.

63 Ibid.

64 Eagleton, *Trouble with Strangers*, 238.

65 Razack, *Dark Threats*, 25.

66 Gilbert and Lo, *Performance and Cosmopolitics*, 204.

67 Ouzounian, "Beyond *KONY 2012*: Canadian Play *SIA* Probes World of African Child Soldiers," *Toronto Star*, 20 March 2012.

68 Brooks, *Melodramatic*, 29.

69 MacKenzie, *SIA*, 22.

70 Ibid., 47.

71 Ibid., 7.

72 Ibid., 39.

73 Ibid., 66.

74 Hoile, "SIA: Innocence Lost," *Stagedoor.com*, http://www.stagedoor.com/Theatre/2012/Entries/2012/3/28_SIA.html.

75 Razack, *Dark Threats*, 26–7.

76 Salverson, "Change," 123.

77 Decker, "Internal Hybrids," 191.

78 Pratt, *Imperial Eyes*, 202.

79 Boltanski, *Distant Suffering*, 5.

80 Lehmann, *Postdramatic*, 185.
81 Corbey, "Ethnographic Showcases," 359.
82 "KONY 2012," *YouTube* video, 29:58, Posted by Invisible Children, https://www.youtube.com /watch?v=Y4MnpzG5Sqc.
83 Boler, "Risks of Empathy," 258.
84 Amin, *Land of Strangers*, 33.
85 Gilbert and Lo, *Cosmopolitics*, 4.
86 See Burvill, "Politics Begins as Ethics,"
87 See Beckett, *Worstword Ho*.
88 Gilbert and Lo, *Cosmopolitics*, 12.
89 Rumford, *Globalization*, 121.

CHAPTER FIVE

1 Willis, "Emancipated Spectatorship," 397.
2 After its 2010 performance in Toronto, *A Taste of Empire* was restaged in Vancouver in the Granville Island Public Market in 2014.
3 Brecht, *Brecht on Theatre*, 179.
4 See Boal, *Theatre of the Oppressed*.
5 Quoted in White, *Audience Participation*, 23.
6 Matthew Reason, "Researching the 'active' theatre audience," *Participations* 12, no. 1, May 2015, http://www.participations.org/Volume%2012/Issue%201/17.pdf.
7 I refuse strict definitions of immersive or participatory theatre here for two reasons: one, because it is the general impulse toward a more "active" ethics among these practices that interests me; and two, because I do not wish to privilege any particular theatrical strategy or dramaturgy as possessing some richer ethical substance.
8 See Rancière, "Emancipated Spectator."
9 See Harvie, *Fair Play*.
10 Zaiontz, "Narcissistic Spectatorship," 411.
11 Lehmann, *Postdramatic*, 186.
12 Ibid., 185.
13 Ibid., 183.
14 Ibid., 185.
15 Ibid.
16 Ibid., 177.
17 Grehan, *Performance*, 22.

18 Willis, "Emancipated Spectatorship," 386.
19 Ibid., 397.
20 White, "Immersive Theatre," 221.
21 Lehmann, *Postdramatic*, 186.
22 It's a Freedom Thing Theatre, *Nightmare/Dream.*
23 Reason, "Researching," 274.
24 Amin, *Land of Strangers*, 29.
25 Massey, *World City*, 193.
26 Lehmann, *Postdramatic*, 185.
27 I experienced Debaj's ability to navigate the local and global first hand when I worked with them on an international theatre exchange project, the *Prague-Toronto-Manitoulin Theatre Project,* which ran from 1998 to 2006. It became the central case study of my doctoral research on intercultural theatre. See Freeman, *Toward a Postmodern Ethnography.*
28 Gómez-Peña and Mendieta, "A Latino Philosopher," 544.
29 Gómez-Peña, *Ethno-Techno*, 52.
30 White, "Immersive Theatre," 222.
31 Lehmann, *Postdramatic*, 186.
32 Bauman, *Does Ethics Have a Chance*, 9.
33 Amin, *Land of Strangers*, 33.
34 Reinelt, "Three Thoughts," 151.
35 Burvill, "Politics Begins as Ethics," 235.
36 See Auslander, *Liveness.*
37 Lehmann, *Postdramatic*, 141.
38 We could add to these another supplied by Julie Salverson, who, in confronting the problem of the "aesthetic of injury" occasioned by "tragic" stagings of strangers, turned to clown technique as a surprising and poignant means of bearing "foolish witness" to tragedy. See Salverson, "Taking Liberties."
39 Ridout, *Ethics*, 66.
40 Ibid.

EPILOGUE

1 Jordan Press, "Details of missing video segment by Ottawa shooter to be released," http://www.theglobeandmail.com/news/politics/ottawa-shooter-missing-video-segment/article24673655/.
2 Twice as many as died in this one terrible incident on the same body of

water in April 2015 alone. See "April 2015 Mediterranean Sea migrant shipwrecks," *Wikipedia*, https://en.wikipedia.org/wiki/April_2015_Mediterranean_Sea_migrant_shipwrecks.

3 Zoe Williams, "Katie Hopkins calling migrants vermin recalls the darkest events of history," http://www.theguardian.com/commentisfree/2015/apr/19/katie-hopkins-migrants-vermin-darkest-history-drownings

4 Anealla Safdar, "Brexit: UKIP's 'unethical' anti-immigration poster," http://www.aljazeera.com/indepth/features/2016/06/brexit-anti-immigration-ukip-poster-raises-questions-160621112722799.html.

5 Boltanski, *Distant Suffering*, 12.

6 Bauman, *In Search of Politics*, 202.

7 Alexander, *Dark Side of Modernity*, 87.

8 Ibid., 100.

9 My thanks to Arianne de Waal at the Ruhr-Universität Bochum for suggesting this phrasing.

10 The British Theatre Consortium, "Critical Mass: Theatre Spectatorship and Value Attribution," http://britishtheatreconference.co.uk/wp-content/uploads/2014/05/Critical-Mass-10.7.pdf.

11 Ibid., 26.

12 Ibid., 29.

13 Matthew Reason, "Researching the 'Active' Theatre Audience," *Participations* 12, no. 1 May 2015, http://www.participations.org/Volume%2012/Issue%201/17.pdf.

14 See Bauman, *Collateral Damage*.

15 Maria Popova, "Philosopher Martha Nussbaum on How to Live with Fragility," http://www.brainpickings.org/2014/03/14/martha-nussbaum-bill-moyers-world-of-ideas/.

Bibliography

Abu-Laban, Yasmeen and Christina Gabriel. *Selling Diversity: Immigration, Multiculturalism, Employment Equity, and Globalization*. Peterborough, Ont.: University of Toronto Press, 2008.

Ahmed, Sara. *Strange Encounters: Embodied Others in Post-Coloniality*. London: Routledge, 2000.

Alexander, Jeffrey C. *The Dark Side of Modernity*. Cambridge: Polity Press, 2013.

Amin, Ash. *Land of Strangers*. Cambridge: Polity Press, 2012.

Appadurai, Arjun. *Modernity at Large: Cultural Dimensions of Globalization*. Minneapolis: University of Minnesota Press, 1996.

Appiah, [Kwame] Anthony. "The Case for Contamination." *New York Times Magazine*, 1 January 2006.

– "Cosmopolitan Patriots." *Critical Inquiry* 23, no. 3 (spring 1997): 617–39.

– *The Ethics of Identity*. Princeton, NJ: Princeton University Press, 2005.

– *Experiments in Ethics*. Cambridge, Mass.: Harvard University Press, 2008.

– *The Politics of Culture, The Politics of Identity*. ICC at the ROM, 2008.

Arendt, Hannah. *On Revolution*. New York: Viking Press, 1965.

Auslander, Philip. *Liveness: Performance in a Mediatized Culture*. London; New York: Routledge, 1999.

Banting, Keith and Will Kymlicka. "Canadian Multiculturalism: Global Anxieties and Local Debates." *British Journal of Canadian Studies* 23, no. 1 (January 2010): 43–72.

Barish, Jonas A. *The Antitheatrical Prejudice*. Berkeley: University of California Press, 1980.

Bauman, Zygmunt. *Collateral Damage: Social Inequalities in a Global Age*. Cambridge: Polity Press, 2011.

– *Community: Seeking Safety in an Insecure World*. Cambridge: Polity Press, 2001.
– *Does Ethics Have a Chance in a World of Consumers?* Cambridge, Mass.: Harvard University Press, 2008.
– *In Search of Politics*. Cambridge: Polity Press, 1999.
– *Liquid Modernity*, Cambridge; Malden, Mass.: Polity Press; Blackwell, 2000.
– "Migration and Identities in the Globalized World." *Philosophy & Social Criticism* 37, no. 4 (May 2011): 425–35.
Strangers at our Door. Cambridge: Polity Press, 2016.
– and Lydia Bauman, *Culture in a Liquid Modern World*. Cambridge; Malden, Mass.: 2011.
Beckett, Samuel. *Worstword Ho*. London: John Calder, 1983.
Berger, Jeniva. "A Coat of Many Colours: The Multicultural Theatre Movement in Canada." In Anton Wagner. ed. *Contemporary Canadian Theatre: New World Visions.* 216–26. Toronto: Simon & Pierre, 1985.
Bharucha, Rustom. "Politics of Culturalisms in an Age of Globalisation: Discrimination, Discontent and Dialogue." *Economic and Political Weekly* 34, no. 8 (1999): 477–89.
Bissoondath, Neil. *Selling Illusions: The Cult of Multiculturalism in Canada*. Toronto: Penguin, 2002.
Boal, Augusto. *Theatre of the Oppressed*. London: Pluto Press, 2008.
Boler, Megan. "The Risks of Empathy: Interrogating Multiculturalism's Gaze." *Cultural Studies* 11, no. 2 (May 1997): 253–73.
Boltanski, Luc. *Distant Suffering: Morality, Media and Politics*. Cambridge; New York: Cambridge University Press, 1999.
Brecht, Bertolt. *Brecht on Theatre: The Development of an Aesthetic*. London: Methuen, 1964.
Brooks, Peter. *The Melodramatic Imagination: Balzac, Henry James, Melodrama, and the Mode of Excess*. New Haven: Yale University Press, 1976.
Bryden, Ronald and Boyd Neil, eds. *Whittaker's Theatre: A Critic Looks at Stages in Canada and Thereabouts, 1944–1975*. Greenbank, Ont.: Whittaker Project, 1985.
Burian, Jarka. *Modern Czech Theatre: Reflector and Conscience of a Nation*. Iowa City: University of Iowa Press, 2000.
Burvill, Tom. "Politics Begins as Ethics: Levinasian Ethics and Australian Performance Concerning Refugees." *Research in Drama Education: The Journal of Applied Theatre and Performance* 13, no. 2 (2008): 233–43.

Butler, Judith. *Frames of War: When Is Life Grievable?* London: Verso, 2009.

Carlson, Marvin. *Speaking in Tongues: Language at Play in the Theatre.* Ann Arbor: University of Michigan Press, 2006.

Castells, Manuel. *End of Millennium*. Malden, Mass.: Wiley-Blackwell, 2010.

Choi, Ins. *Kim's Convenience*. Toronto: House of Anansi, 2012.

Corbey, Raymond. "Ethnographic Showcases, 1870–1930," *Cultural Anthropology* 8, no. 3 (1993): 338–69.

Crenshaw, Kimberlé Williams. "Mapping the Margins: Intersectionality, Identity Politics, and Violence against Women of Color." *Stanford Law Review* 43, no. 6 (July 1991): 1241–99.

Čermák, Josef. *It All Began with Prince Rupert: The Story of Czechs and Slovaks in Canada.* Czech Republic: Atelier IM Pub. Co. Luhačovice, 2005.

Davis, Walter A. *Art and Politics: Psychoanalysis, Ideology, Theatre*. London: Pluto Press, 2007.

Decker, Christof. "Internal Hybrids: The Westerner as Melodramatic Victim." In Ralph J. Poole and Ilke Saal, eds., *Passionate Politics: The Cultural Work of American Melodrama from the Early Republic to the Present.* 187–212. Newcastle, UK: Cambridge Scholars, 2008.

Di Giovanni, Caroline. "The Ontario Multicultural Theatre Association: The First decade, 1971–81." *Polyphony* (Bulletin of the Multicultural History Society of Ontario) 5, no. 2 (fall/winter 1983): 112–17.

Dolan, Jill. *The Feminist Spectator as Critic*. Ann Arbor: University of Michigan Press, 2012.

Doucet, Michael J. "Anatomy of an Urban Legend: Toronto's Multicultural Reputation." *Ceris: Joint Centre of Excellence for Research on Immigration and Settlement*, April 2001.

DuBois, W.E.B. *The Souls of Black Folk*. New York; Avenel, NJ: Gramercy Books, 1994.

Eagleton, Terry. *Trouble with Strangers: A Study of Ethics*. Chichester; Malden, Mass.: Wiley-Blackwell, 2009.

Filewod, Alan. "Erasing Historical Difference: The Alternative Orthodoxy in Canadian Theatre." *Theatre Journal* 42, no. 1 (1989): 201–10.

Freeman, Barry. "Navigating the Prague-Toronto-Manitoulin Theatre Project: A Postmodern Ethnographic Approach to Intercultural Theatre." *Theatre Research in Canada* 30, no. 1–2 (2009): 58–81.

– "The Social Neuroscience of Empathy in the Theatre of Global Ethics." *Performing Ethos* 2, no. 1. 41–54.

– *Toward a Postmodern Ethnography of Intercultural Theatre: An Instrumental*

Case-Study of the Prague-Toronto-Manitoulin Theatre Project. (2010). http://hdl.handle.net/1807/24752.

Ghazali, Ahmed. *The Sheep and the Whale.* Bobby Theodore, trans. Unpublished.

Giddens, Anthony. *Modernity and Self-Identity: Self and Society in the Late Modern Age*. Cambridge: Polity Press, 1991.

– *Runaway World: How Globalisation Is Reshaping Our Lives*. London: Profile Books, 1999.

Gilbert, Helen and Jacqueline Lo, *Performance and Cosmopolitics: Cross-Cultural Transactions in Australasia.* Basingstoke, Hampshire; New York: Palgrave Macmillan, 2007.

Gluhovic, Milija. "Too Distant Shores: The Strait of Gibraltar and the Space of Exception." *Research in Drama Education: Journal of Applied Theatre and Performance* 13, no. 2: 147–58

Goetz-Stankiewicz, Marketa. *The Silenced Theatre: Czech Playwrights without a Stage*. Toronto: University of Toronto Press, 1979.

Grehan, Helena. *Performance, Ethics and Spectatorship in a Global Age*. Basingstoke, Hampshire; New York: Palgrave Macmillan, 2009.

Gómez-Peña, Guillermo. *Ethno-Techno: Writings on Performance, Activism, and Pedagogy*. New York: Routledge, 2005.

– and Eduardo Mendieta, "A Latino Philosopher Interviews a Chicano Performance Artist." *Nepantla: Views from South* 2, no. 3 (2001): 539–54.

Grosz, E.A. *Space, Time, and Perversion: Essays on the Politics of Bodies*. New York: Routledge, 1995.

Gutsell, Jennifer and Michael Inzlicht, "Empathy Constrained: Prejudice Predicts Reduced Mental Simulation of Actions during Observation of Out-groups." *Journal of American Social Psychology* 46: 841–5.

Hardt, Michael and Antonio Negri, *Empire*. Cambridge, Mass.: Harvard University Press, 2000.

Harney, Robert F. "The Ethnic Press in Ontario." *Polyphony* (Bulletin of the Multicultural History Society of Ontario) 4, no. 1 (spring/summer 1982): 1–2.

– "Immigrant Theatre." *Polyphony* (Bulletin of the Multicultural History Society of Ontario) 5, no. 2 (fall/winter 1983): 1–14.

Harvie, Jen. *Fair Play: Art, Performance and Neoliberalism*. Basingstoke, Hampshire; New York: Palgrave Macmillan, 2013.

– and Richard Paul Knowles, "Herbert Whittaker, Reporting from the

Front: *Montreal Gazette*, 1937–1949, and *Globe and Mail*, 1949–1975." In Anton Wagner, ed. *Establishing Our Boundaries: English-Canadian Theatre Criticism*. 215–33. Toronto: University of Toronto Press, 1999.

Heelas, Paul, Scott Lash, and Paul Morris, eds. *Detraditionalization: Critical Reflections on Authority and Identity*. Cambridge, Mass.: Blackwell Publishers, 1996.

Hernandez, Catherine. *Singkil*. Toronto: Playwrights Canada Press, 2009.

Hodkinson, Yvonne. *Female Parts: The Art and Politics of Women Playwrights*. Montreal: Black Rose Books, 1991.

Holledge, Julie and Joanne Tompkins. *Women's Intercultural Performance*. London; New York: Routledge, 2000.

It's a Freedom Thing Theatre. *Nightmare/Dream*. Unpublished.

Janover, Michael. "Nostalgias." *Critical Horizons* 1, no. 1 (2000): 113–33.

Kahneman, Daniel and Amos Tversky, "Prospect theory: An Analysis of Decision under Risk." *Econometrica* 47: 263–91.

Kamboureli, Smaro. *Scandalous Bodies: Diasporic Literature in English Canada*. Waterloo, Ont.: Wilfrid Laurier University Press, 2009.

Kaplan, Amy. "Manifest Domesticity." *American Literature: A Journal of Literary History, Criticism, and Bibliography* 70, 3 (1998): 581–606.

Kearney, Richard and Kascha Semonovitch. *Phenomenologies of the Stranger: Between Hostility and Hospitality*. New York: Fordham University Press, 2011.

King, Robert L. *The Ethos of Drama: Rhetorical Theory and Dramatic Worth*. Washington, DC: Catholic University of America Press, 2010.

Kitcher, Philip. *The Ethical Project*. Cambridge, Mass.: Harvard University Press, 2011.

Knowles, Richard Paul. *How Theatre Means*. New York: Palgrave Macmillan, 2014.

– *Reading the Material Theatre*. Cambridge; New York: Cambridge University Press, 2004.

– *Theatre & Interculturalism*. Basingstoke, UK; New York: Palgrave Macmillan, 2010.

Lehmann, Hans-Thies. *Postdramatic Theatre*. London; New York: Routledge, 2006.

Lei, Daphne. "Homeland under Attack: Looking for a New Theatrical Paradigm in Asian Americas." In Nina Lee Aquino and Ric Knowles, eds. *Asian Canadian Theatre*. 33–48. Toronto: Playwrights Canada Press, 2011.

Lifton, Robert J. *Death in Life: Survivors of Hiroshima.* New York: Random House, 1987.

Li, Peter S. *The Chinese in Canada*. Toronto: Oxford University Press, 1988.

– "A World Apart: The Multicultural World of Visible Minorities and the Art World of Canada." *The Canadian Review of Sociology and Anthropology* 31, no. 4 (November 1994): 365–91.

Lo, Jacqueline and Helen Gilbert, "Toward a Topography of Cross-Cultural Theatre Praxis," *Drama Review* 46, no. 3 (fall 2002): 31–53.

MacKenzie, Matt. *SIA*. Unpublished.

Mackey, Clarke. *Random Acts of Culture: Reclaiming Art and Community in the 21st Century.* Toronto: Between the Lines, 2010.

Massey, Doreen. *World City*. Cambridge; Malden, Mass: Polity Press, 2007.

– David Featherstone, and Sophie Bond. "The Possibilities of a Politics of Place Beyond Place? A Conversation with Doreen Massey." *Scottish Geographical Journal* 125, no. 3 (September 2009): 401–20.

Maufort, Marc. *Transgressive Itineraries: Postcolonial Hybridizations of Dramatic Realism*. New York: P.I.E.-Peter Lang, 2003.

McKinnie, Michael. *City Stages: Theatre and Urban Space in a Global City.* Toronto: University of Toronto Press, 2007.

– "Performing the Civic Transnational: Cultural Production, Governance, and Citizenship in Contemporary London." In *Performance and the City.* 110–27. New York: Palgrave Macmillan, 2009.

Negt, Oskar. *Public Sphere and Experience: Toward an Analysis of the Bourgeois and Proletarian Public Sphere*. Minneapolis: University of Minnesota Press, 1993.

Nussbaum, Martha C. *The Fragility of Goodness: Luck and Ethics in Greek Tragedy and Philosophy.* New York: Cambridge University Press, 1987.

Off, Carol. "Heritage or Cultural Evolution: Federal Policy on Multiculturalism and the Arts." *Canadian Theatre Review* 56 (fall 1988): 5–8.

Ornstein, Robert E. *New World New Mind: Moving toward Conscious Evolution.* New York: Simon & Schuster, 1990.

Overton, James. *Making a World of Difference: Essays on Tourism, Culture and Development in Newfoundland*. St. John's, Nfld.: ISER Books, 1996.

Petroff, Lillian. "Prosperity and Patriotism: Macedonian Theatre in Toronto 1910–1940." *Polyphony* (Bulletin of the Multicultural History Society of Ontario) 5, no. 2 (fall/winter 1983): 81–3.

Phelan, Shane. *Sexual Strangers: Gays, Lesbians and Dilemmas of Citizenship*. Philadelphia, Pa.: Temple University Press, 2001.

Piketty, Thomas. *Capital in the Twenty-First Century*. Cambridge, Mass.: Belknap Press of Harvard University Press, 2014.

Pinker, Steven. *The Better Angels of Our Nature: Why Violence Has Declined*. New York: Viking, 2011.

Pratt, Mary Louise. *Imperial Eyes: Travel Writing and Transculturation*, 2nd ed. London; New York: Routledge, 2008.

Quan, Betty. *Mother Tongue.* Montreal: Scirocco Drama, 1996.

Rae, Paul. "Where Is the Cosmopolitan Stage?" *Contemporary Theatre Review* 16, no. 1 (2006): 8–22.

Rancière, Jacques. "The Emancipated Spectator," *Artforum International*, March 2007.

Razack, Sherene. *Dark Threats and White Knights: The Somalia Affair, Peacekeeping, and the New Imperialism*. Toronto: University of Toronto Press, 2004.

Reinelt, Janelle. "Three Thoughts toward a Global Poetics." *Contemporary Theatre Review* 16, no. 1 (2006): 150–2.

Rewa, Natalie. "Theatre and Ethnicity." *Canadian Theatre Review* 56 (fall 1988): 3.

Ridout, Nicholas. *Theatre and Ethics.* New York: Palgrave Macmillan, 2009.

Rodgers, Jenna. "Manipulating Theatrical Space to Create Physical Place: Betty Quan's *Mother Tongue* Reclaiming Space for the Individual." In Nina Lee Aquino and Ric Knowles, eds. *Asian Canadian Theatre.* 171–82. Toronto: Playwrights Canada Press, 2011.

Rumford, Chris. *The Globalization of Strangeness*. New York: Palgrave Macmillan, 2013.

Rut, Přemysl. "The State of the Czech Theatre," *New Theatre Quarterly* 27 (August 1991): 289–91.

Safertal, Frank J. and Pavel Král, "It All Started with Adolf … A Short History of Toronto's New Theatre (Nové divadlo)." In Vera Borkovec, *Czech and Slovak Theatre Abroad: In the USA, Canada, Australia and England*, 1st ed. 51–66. Boulder, Col.; New York: East European Monographs; Columbia University Press, 2006.

Salverson, Julie. "Change on Whose Terms? Testimony and an Erotics of Inquiry." *Theater* 31, no. 3 (2001): 119–25.

– "Taking Liberties: A Theatre Class of Foolish Witness." *Research in Drama Education: Journal of Applied Theatre and Performance* 13, no. 2: 245–55.

Sayer, Derek. *The Coasts of Bohemia: A Czech History*. Princeton, NJ: Princeton University Press, 1998.

– *Prague, Capital of the Twentieth Century: A Surrealist History*. Princeton, NJ: Princeton University Press, 2013.

Schellekens, Elisabeth. *Aesthetics and Morality*. New York: Continuum, 2007.

Schonberg, Michal Quentin. *The Osvobozené divadlo of Voskovec and Werich: A History – The Liberated Theatre of Voskovec and Werich*. Toronto: s.n, 1977).

Scott, Shelley. *Nightwood Theatre: A Woman's Work Is Always Done*. Edmonton: AU Press, 2010.

Singer, Ben. *Melodrama and Modernity: Early Sensational Cinema and Its Contexts*. New York: Columbia University Press, 2001.

Singer, Peter. *One World: The Ethics of Globalization*. New Haven, Conn.: Yale University Press, 2002.

Singer, Tania et al. "A Common Role of Insula in Feelings, Empathy and Uncertainty." *Trends in Cognitive Sciences* 13, no. 8 (2010): 334–40.

Slovic, Paul. "If I Look at the Mass I Will Never Act: Psychic Numbing and Genocide." *Judgment and Decision Making* 2: 79–85.

Smith, James Leslie. *Melodrama*. London: Methuen, 1973.

Stefura, Mary. "Aspects of Culture in the Ukrainian Community of the Sudbury Area." *Polyphony* (Bulletin of the Multicultural History Society of Ontario) 5, no. 2 (fall/winter 1983): 29–32.

Škvorecký, Josef. *Bůh do domu: Fraška O Čtyřech Dějstvích*. Toronto: Sixty-Eight Publishers, 1980.

Taylor, Charles. *Multiculturalism: Examining the Politics of Recognition*. Princeton, NJ: Princeton University Press, 1994.

Theatrefront. *RETURN: The Sarajevo Project*. Toronto: Playwrights Canada Press, 2007.

Thobani, Sunera. *Exalted Subjects: Studies in the Making of Race and Nation in Canada*. Buffalo: University of Toronto Press, 2007.

Till, Chris, and Tom Campbell, "Resistance Towards Ethics." In *Bauman's Challenge: Sociological Issues for the 21st Century*. 172–88. New York: Palgrave Macmillan, 2010.

Tomovic, Vladislav. "Theatre among the Serbs, Croats and Slovenes." *Polyphony* (Bulletin of the Multicultural History Society of Ontario) 5, no. 2 (fall/winter 1983): 75–7.

Trask, Bahira Sherif. *Globalization and Families: Accelerated Systemic Social Change*. New York: Springer, 2010.

Trout, J.D. *The Empathy Gap: Building Bridges to the Good Life and the Good Society*. New York: Viking, 2009.

Ty, Eleanor. "Affect, Family, and the Past in Two Plays by Catherine Hernandez." In Nina Lee Aquino and Ric Knowles, eds. *Asian Canadian Theatre.* 212–22. Toronto: Playwrights Canada Press, 2011.

Varma, Rahul. *Bhopal*. Toronto: Playwrights Canada Press, 2005.

Willis, Emma. "Emancipated Spectatorship and Subjective Drift: Understanding the Work of the Spectator in Erik Ehn's Soulographie." *Theatre Journal* 66, no. 3 (2014): 384–404.

White, Gareth. *Audience Participation in Theatre: Aesthetics of the Invitation*. Basingstoke, Hampshire: Palgrave Macmillan, 2013.

– "On Immersive Theatre." *Theatre Research International* 37, no. 3 (2012): 221–35.

Wolfe, Kurt H., ed. *The Sociology of Georg Simmel*. New York: Collier MacMillan Publishers, 1950.

Wynnyckyj, Iroida L. "Amateur Theatre in Canadian Ukrainian Community Halls." *Polyphony* (Bulletin of the Multicultural History Society of Ontario) 5, no. 2 (fall/winter 1983): 87–94.

Yhap, Beverly. "On Their Own Terms." *Canadian Theatre Review* 56 (fall 1998): 25–8.

Zaiontz, Keren. "Narcissistic Spectatorship in Immersive and One-on-One Performance." *Theatre Journal* 66, no. 3 (2014): 405–25.

Žižek, Slavoj. "Multiculturalism, or, the Cultural Logic of Multinational Capitalism." *New Left Review* 225 (September 1997). n.p.

Index

Page numbers with (i) refer to illustrations.